Key Questions

'O' Level Physics MCQs

First edition

ISBN 978-1-105-28138-9
90000

9 781105 281389

Contents

Introduction

This book was written for motivated students with a desire to excel.

This collection of questions follows the latest 'O' Level syllabus closely. It is meant to be used as a guide to aid students in the thorough understanding of 'O' Level Chemistry.

Here's wishing you an enjoyable learning journey.

Please contact me at l.han.07@gmail.com should you have any feedback. It will be very much appreciated. Thank you very much.

1 Measurement of Physical Quantities [__ / 30]

1. Which is correct?

	Scalar	Vector
a.	Displacement	Velocity
b.	Length	Mass
c.	Distance	Acceleration
d.	Weight	Mass

2. Which statement would you not agree with?
   a. A vernier calipers is less precise than a micrometer screw gauge
   b. A vernier calipers can measure internal diameters whereas a micrometer screw gauge cannot
   c. Both vernier calipers and micrometer screw gauges are subject to zero errors
   d. A vernier calipers only has positive zero errors whereas a micrometer screw gauge can have both negative as well as positive zero errors

3. Which statement about cotton wool and lead is correct?
   a. 1kg of cotton wool has less mass than 1kg of lead
   b. 1kg of cotton wool has the same mass as 1kg of lead
   c. 2kg of cotton wool has the same mass as 1kg of lead
   d. 1kg of cotton wool has the same density as 1kg of lead

4. A pendulum's period can be increased by
   a. Using a pendulum of a larger mass
   b. Using a pendulum of a larger density
   c. Using a longer string
   d. Using a round pendulum instead of a flat one

5. Which is denser, steel ball X or steel cube Y?

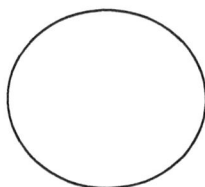

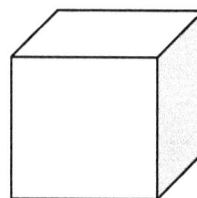

    a.   Steel ball X
    b.   Steel cube Y
    c.   Both have the same density
    d.   It is impossible to tell

6. A micrometer screw gauge shows the following reading when closed. What is the negative zero error?

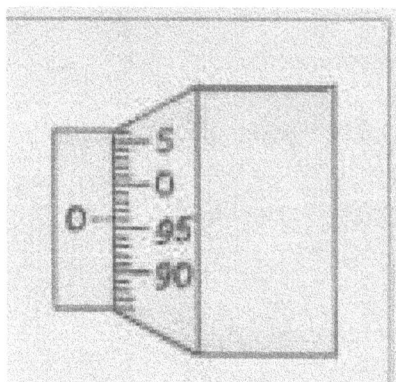

    a.   0.96 mm
    b.   0.96 cm
    c.   0.04 cm
    d.   0.04 mm

7. The micrometer screw gauge is used to measure the diameter of a pencil. It shows this reading:

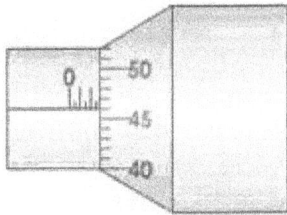

What is the diameter of the pencil?
   a. 2.46 mm
   b. 2.96 mm
   c. 2.46 cm
   d. 2.96 cm

8. A student wants to use the instrument used in the previous question to measure the diameter of a cup. Do you think it is a good choice?
   a. Yes, because it is very accurate
   b. No, because it is not accurate enough
   c. Yes, because the cup is too small
   d. No, because the cup is too wide

9. Which measurement is not necessary to determine the density of an object?
   a. Mass
   b. Volume
   c. Length
   d. Gravitational field strength

10. What will happen to the period of a pendulum when it is brought up to the moon from earth?
   a. It increases
   b. It decreases
   c. It does not change
   d. It becomes zero

11. A simple pendulum swings from the extreme left to the extreme right and back to the extreme left 10 times. It takes 1 minute for the entire process. What is its period and frequency?

    a.   10 s, 0.1 Hz
    b.   0.1s, 10 Hz
    c.   6 s, 0.17 Hz
    d.   0.17 s, 6 Hz

12. A block of metal sinks in water, but a ship built from the same metal floats on water. Why?

    a.   The ship has a higher volume:mass ratio
    b.   The metal has a lower density when used to make a ship
    c.   The block has a lower mass:volume ratio
    d.   The metal has a lower density when used to form a block

13. The following shapes are cut out from a piece of wood. Which statement is true?

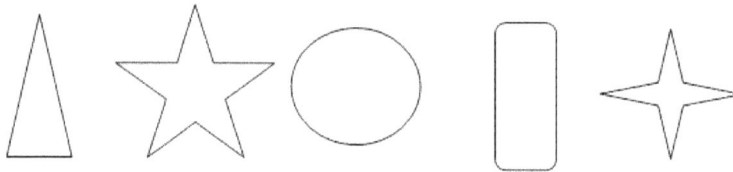

    a.   They have the same surface area
    b.   They have the same weight
    c.   They have the same density
    d.   They have the same mass

14. A string of wool is wound 500 times around a knitting rod. The length of rod covered by the wool is 5cm. What is the radius of the string of wool?

    a.   0.1mm
    b.   0.01mm
    c.   0.05mm
    d.   0.005mm

15. A closed vernier calipers show the following reading when closed.

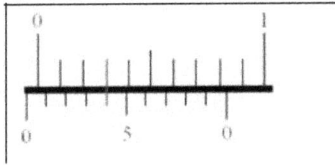

What can be inferred from this?
a. It is negative zero error
b. It is a positive zero error
c. There is no zero error
d. The zero error is + 0.03 cm

16. A ball is placed between the jaws of the instrument in the previous question. It shows the following reading. What is the radius of the ball?

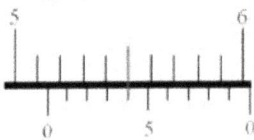

a. 5.15 mm
b. 5.18 mm
c. 5.15 cm
d. 5.18 cm

17. Another ball of radius twice that of the first ball is placed between the jaws of the vernier calipers. What is the reading shown?
a. 10.30 mm
b. 20.60 mm
c. 10.30 cm
d. 20.60 cm

18. A 0.8kg stone is lowered into a displacement can. A volume of water is displaced and poured into a measuring cylinder. The reading is as shown below.

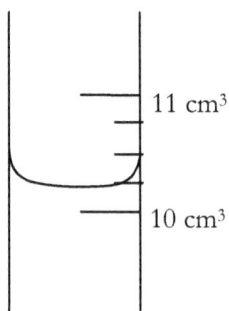

11 cm³

10 cm³

What is the volume of water that has been displaced?
a. 10.10 cm³
b. 10.20 cm³
c. 10.25 cm³
d. 10.40 cm³

19. What is the density (in SI units) of the stone in the previous question?
a. 0.8 / vol
b. 0.8 / (vol/100³)
c. 800 / vol
d. 800 / (vol/100³)

20. The same stone is lowered into another displacement can containing liquid X instead of water. Liquid X has a higher density than water. Jo records the volume of liquid X displaced as 10.00 cm², Joan records it as 10.25 cm², and Joanna records it as 10.50 cm². Who is correct, and why?
a. Joan, because the volume recorded is not affected by the density of the liquid
b. Joan, because the volume recorded is supposed to decrease
c. Joanna, because the volume recorded is supposed to increase
d. None of the are correct, because the volume recorded is supposed to increase

21. What will happen to the frequency of a pendulum when it is brought up a mountain?
a. It increases
b. It decreases
c. It does not change
d. It becomes zero

22. A simple pendulum takes 5s to swing from the extreme left to the extreme right. What is its period and frequency?
    a. 10 s, 0.1 Hz
    b. 0.1s, 10 Hz
    c. 5 s, 0.2 Hz
    d. 0.1s, 5 Hz

23. 2 similar copper balls are placed one at sea level and the other on the top of a mountain. Which statement is true when comparing the ball at sea level to the ball on the top of the mountain?
    a. It has a smaller volume because there is more atmospheric pressure acting on it
    b. It has a smaller mass because there is more atmospheric pressure acting on it
    c. It has a lower density because it is at a lower height from the earth
    d. It has a larger weight because it is at a lower height from the earth

24. Arrange in order of increasing density: object X, object Y, liquid Z

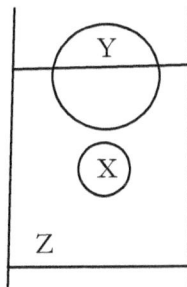

    a. Y, X, Z
    b. Z, X, Y
    c. Y, X Z
    d. X Z, Y

25. An iron pendulum bob has a period of T. It is replaced with a plastic bob of half the mass but same size and shape. What is the new period?
    a. 0.25 T
    b. 0.5 T
    c. T
    d. 2 T

26. Why is it easy to maintain balance while on a smoothly moving train but difficult to maintain balance on a jerky train?
    a. Because of inertia
    b. Because of gravity
    c. Because of friction
    d. Because of electricity

27. Why do people sink in water but float in the dead sea?
    a. The salt in the dead sea makes the water denser than pure water
    b. The salt in the dead sea makes the water less dense than pure water
    c. The geographical location of the dead sea has higher gravitational force
    d. The geographical location of the dead sea has lower gravitational force

28. A freely falling ball that bounces off the ground is able to reach a much higher height on the moon than on the earth. True or false?
    a. True, because gravity on the moon is weaker
    b. True, because the moon's surface is more elactic
    c. False, because gravity on the moon is weaker
    d. False, because gravity does not affect the height

29. Which list contains only vectors?
    a. Velocity, time, distance
    b. Work done, current, acceleration
    c. Force, acceleration, weight
    d. Weight, displacement, energy

30. How many scalars are in the following list? Force, density, mass, energy.
    a. 0
    b. 1
    c. 2
    d. 3

2 Kinematics [__ / 30]

1. A man runs from point A to point B that is 50m to the east of point A. He then runs to point C, which is 150m to the west of point A. What is his final displacement?

    a. 200m
    b. 250m
    c. -150m
    d. -200m

2. What is the total distance travelled by the man in question 1?

    a. 150m
    b. 200m
    c. 250m
    d. -250m

3. A car starts from rest and moves with constant acceleration for 10s. It then moves with a constant velocity of 80 km/h before slowing to a stop with constant deceleration of 15km/h^2. Sketch the velocity-time graph of the car's motion.

a.

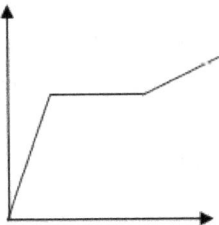

c.

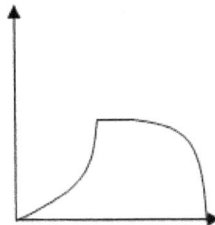

b.

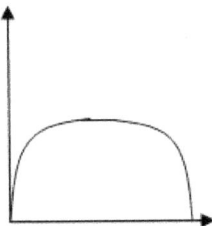

d.

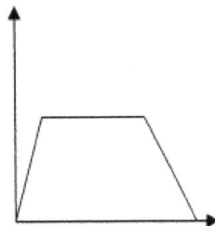

4. Sketch the displacement-time graph of the motion of the car in the previous question.

a.

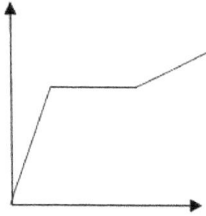

c.

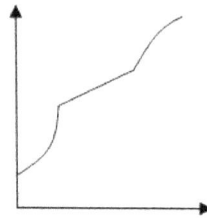

b.

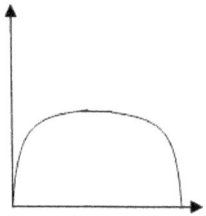

d.

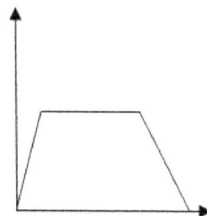

5. Which of the following statements about acceleration is true?
    a.   The acceleration-time graph shows the gradient of the speed-time graph
    b.   The acceleration-time graph shows the area under the speed-time graph
    c.   The acceleration-time graph shows the gradient of the velocity-time graph
    d.   The acceleration-time graph shows the area under the velocity-time graph

6. How long did the car (in the previous question) take to stop?
    a.   1.5s
    b.   5.33 s
    c.   8.25 s
    d.   12 s

7. Ball Y undergoes free fall for twice as long as ball X. How much further does ball Y travel than ball X?
   a. They travel the same distance
   b. Y travels twice the distance of X
   c. Y travels four times the distance of X
   d. Y travels ten times the distance of X

8. Ball X is dropped from rest and falls freely for 5 seconds. The total distance it travels is
   a. Impossible to tell
   b. 5 m
   c. 12.5 m
   d. 25 m

9. The velocity-time graph below shows the movement of car X and car Y from the same point.

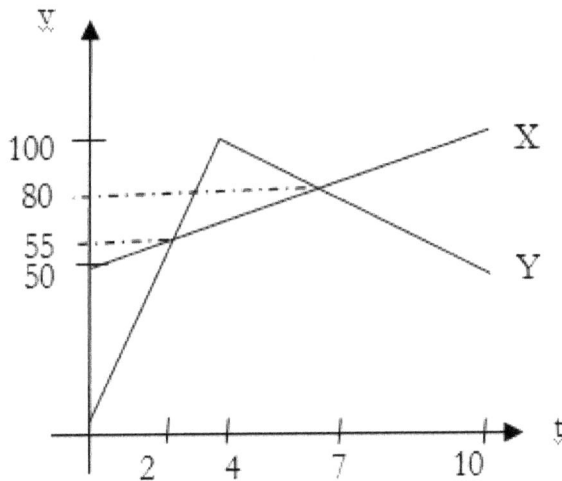

At which points are both cars traveling at the same speed?

   a. 0 s and 10 s
   b. 2 s and 7 s
   c. 55 s and 80 s
   d. 0 s and 4 s

10. Continuing from the question above, what are the accelerations of X and Y at these two points?
    a. 5 ms^{-2} for both cars
    b. 5 ms^{-2} and 25 ms^{-2} respectively
    c. 25 ms^{-2} and 5 ms^{-2} respectively
    d. 5 ms^{-2} and - 25 ms^{-2} respectively

11. Continuing from the question above, what is the difference in distance traveled by the cars?
    a. Car Y traveled 100 m further
    b. Car X traveled 100 m further
    c. Car X traveled 500 m further
    d. Car Y traveled 500 m further

12. Ball X is dropped from the top of a 10 storey building. Ball Y is dropped from the middle of the same building. What is the same for both ball X and ball Y?
    a. Acceleration
    b. Time taken to hit the ground
    c. Final velocity before they hit the ground
    d. Displacement

13. A man starts from rest and runs with a steadily increasing velocity. After 10 seconds, he passes point X with a velocity of 50m/s. How far is point X from his starting point?
    a. 50m
    b. 200m
    c. 250m
    d. 500m

14. If a velocity has a negative value, what does it mean?
    a. The object is moving extremely slowly
    b. The object is moving in the opposite direction
    c. The object is not moving
    d. There must be a force acting on the object

15. A trolley at the middle of a frictionless slope is given an initial push up the slope. It moves up, and then rolls back down. Sketch the velocity time graph of the trolley and indicate

a.

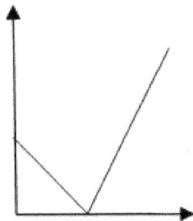

c.

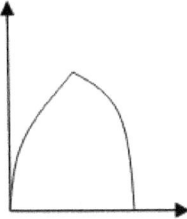

b.

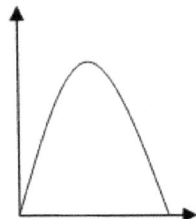

d.

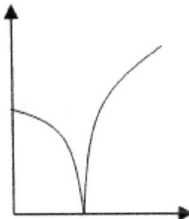

16. How can the displacement of the trolley in the previous question be found using the graph?
    a. Gradient of the graph
    b. The average of the graph's gradients
    c. Area under the graph
    d. Area above the graph

17. A stone is thrown with a velocity of 10m/s to a person standing 5m vertically above. What is the velocity of the stone when the man catches it?
    a. 0 m/s
    b. 14.14 m/s
    c. 20 m/s
    d. 5 m/s

18. A car rolls down a hill from rest. If it travels 50m in the first 5 seconds, what is its acceleration?

　　4 m/s²

　　10 m/s²

　　− 10 m/s²

　　− 4 m/s²

19. A ball is dropped from rest. It falls to the ground and bounces back up. It continues bouncing. Assuming no air resistance, what will the velocity-time graph look like?
    a. Many curved lines, each getting progressively shorter
    b. Many curved lines, all of the same length
    c. Many straight lines, each getting progressively shorter
    d. Many straight lines, all of the same length

20. How would you find the total distance traveled by the ball from the graph you have drawn?
    a. Area under graph
    b. Gradient of graph
    c. Area above graph
    d. Not possible to find the distance traveled using this graph

21. What is the total displacement of the ball?
    a. Zero, because it finally comes to a rest
    b. The distance between the ball's initial position and the ground
    c. The total distance that the ball has bounced
    d. Infinity, because it is impossible to calculate

22. What can be concluded from this velocity time graph?

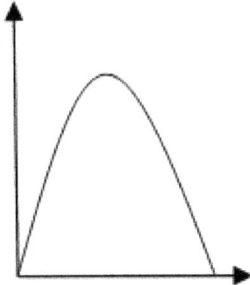

    a.   The car changes direction halfway through the journey
    b.   The car accelerates uniformly and then decelerates uniformly
    c.   The car is moving in a single direction
    d.   The car stops in the middle of the journey and then continues on

23. A car accelerates uniformly from rest to 20 km/h in 5 seconds. What is its displacement?
    a.   0 m
    b.   4 m
    c.   50 m
    d.   100 m

24. A car decelerates uniformly to rest in 7 seconds. It covers a distance of 21 m. What was its velocity?
    a.   3 m/s
    b.   6 m/s
    c.   - 3 m/s
    d.   - 6 m/s

25. The arm of a ticker tape timer vibrates such that it punches a hole in a strip of paper every 0.2s. If the distance between the 1st hole and the 27th hole is 20cm, what is the speed of the timer?
    a. 3.85 m/s
    b. 4.00 m/s
    c. 10 m/s
    d. 100 m/s

26. A runner runs 2 rounds around this track. The two ends are semicircles of radius 20m. The sides are 100m. What is his displacement?

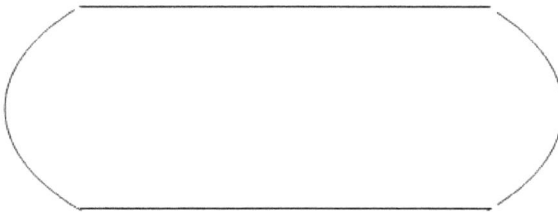

    a. 0 m
    b. 1457 m
    c. 2913 m
    d. 5234 m

27. If he ran at a constant speed, what was also constant?
    a. Velocity
    b. Distance
    c. Acceleration
    d. Deceleration

28. The velocity time graph of car X has a steeper gradient than car Y. What must be true?
    a. Car X is moving at a faster speed
    b. Car X has covered more distance
    c. Car Y is decelerating
    d. Car Y is moving at a lower acceleration

29. The displacement time graph of car X is a curve while the displacement time graph of car Y is a straight line. Which statement is false?
    a. It could be that Car Y is not moving
    b. It could be that Car Y is moving at constant velocity
    c. It can be concluded that car X is moving at non-constant acceleration
    d. It can be concluded that car X is moving at non-constant velocity

30. Which statement is true?
    a. A displacement time graph must always be positive
    b. A velocity time graph can cannot be entirely negative
    c. If a velocity time graph is a curve, the acceleration is uniform
    d. A distance time graph cannot be negative

3 Forces [__ / 45]

1. Choose the most accurate statement.
    a. A moving object must have a net force acting on it
    b. A resting object and a moving object can have the same force acting on it
    c. A resting object has no forces acting on it
    d. A moving object can be made to move faster without changing the forces acting on it

2. Which of the following can never be the resultant of two forces of 2N and 7N?
    a. -9N
    b. 0N
    c. 9N
    d. 14N

3. Which statement about vector diagrams is false?
    a. They can be used to determine the resultant direction of 2 forces
    b. They can be used to determine the resultant magnitude of 2 forces
    c. They can be used for any number of forces
    d. They can be used to add but not subtract forces

4. An 2kg object moves with an acceleration of 3ms^{-2}. It is being pushed with a force of 7N. What is the friction it is experiencing?
    a. 0N
    b. 1N
    c. 2N
    d. 7N

5. Which diagram most accurately shows the resultant of 2 forces?

a.

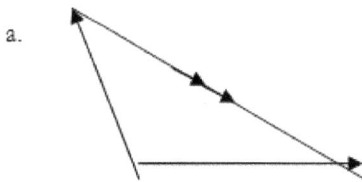

c.

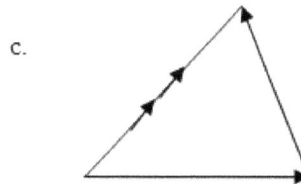

b.

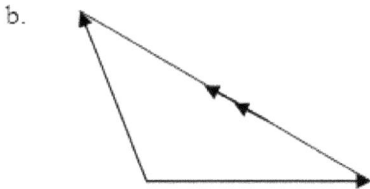

d.

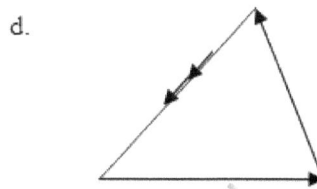

6. When does terminal velocity occur?
   a. When the mass of an object is constant
   b. When an extreme force is acting on an object
   c. When the acceleration of the object is larger than 10 m/s^2
   d. When the resultant force acting on the object is zero

7. A block is kept moving at a constant velocity of 20ms^{-1} by a constant force of 7N. What happens when this force is suddenly removed?
   a. The block suddenly stops moving
   b. The block continues moving with a constant velocity
   c. The block slowly decelerates to rest
   d. The block starts moving in the opposite direction

8. A moving car experiences a frictional force of 100N. Its velocity varies with time as shown below. Choose the most accurate statement about the forward driving force.

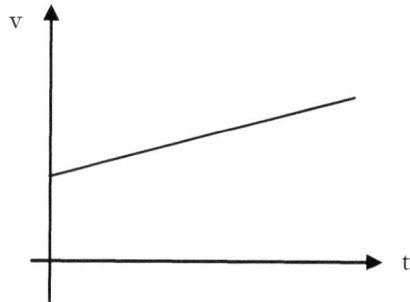

   a. It is zero
   b. It is constant but not zero
   c. It is increasing
   d. It is impossible to tell

9. Two similar loads hang on a frictionless pulley. The string has a negligible mass. What happens?

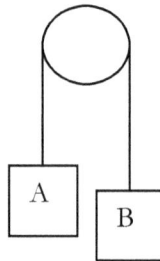

   a. A moves down
   b. B moves up
   c. Nothing happens
   d. B moves down

10. A block moves with constant velocity. The frictional force experienced by the block is 2N. The pulling force is 3N. What is happening?
    a. There is an air resistance force of 1N
    b. There is an air resistance force of 2N
    c. There is an air resistance force of 3N
    d. There is an air resistance force of 5N

11. A van is moving at constant velocity of 65 km/h on a road. Its mass is 500 kg. What is the resultant force acting on it?
    a. 0 N
    b. 7.69 N
    c. 32.5 N
    d. 5000 N

12. If the friction experienced by its wheels is 200 N, find the force provided by the van's engine.
    a. 5000 N
    b. 200 N
    c. 7.69 N
    d. 32.5 N

13. What is the power of the van's engine?
    a. 1 000 W
    b. 3 600 W
    c. 10 000 W
    d. 13 000W

14. The driver steps harder on the accelerator and the engine's force increases by 200 N. What was his speed after 1 min?
    a. 6m/s
    b. 42 m/s
    c. 50 m/s
    d. 89 m/s

15. He reaches his destination in 1 min. How far was he from his destination?
    a. 72 m
    b. 144 m
    c. 720 m
    d. 1 440 m

16. A man jumps from a helicopter. He waits 10 seconds before opening his parachute. Describe what happens to his speed throughout his entire fall.
    a. It increases gradually and suddenly drops to zero
    b. It increases gradually, suddenly drops and then is constant but non-zero
    c. It is constant and then suddenly drops to zero
    d. It is constant and then suddenly decelerates to zero

17. His initial velocity was 120 km/h. What was the distance he fell before he opened his parachute?
    a. 120 m
    b. 500 m
    c. 1000 m
    d. 1200 m

18. A cart is moving along a frictionless surface. A force of 30 N is applied to it for 2 s. If the mass of the cart is 10 kg and it was initially moving at a speed of 10 ms^{-2}, find the speed of the cart immediately after the force is removed.
    a. 3 m/s
    b. 15 m/s
    c. 16 m/s
    d. 30 m/s

19. Forces A and B are 10N and 20N respectively. They lie on a single line. Which of the following is true about the magnitude of their resultant force?

	Maximum	Minimum
a.	30N	-30N
b.	30N	-10N
c.	20N	0N
d.	20N	10N

20. A hanging toy is made of 3 blocks as shown below. The masses of A, B and C are 1kg, 4kg and 7kg respectively. What is the tension in the string between blocks A and B?

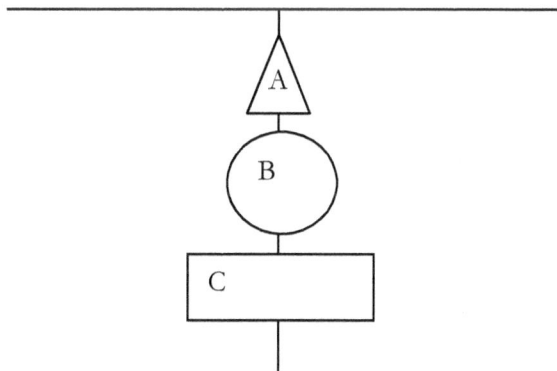

   a. 10N
   b. 11N
   c. 110N
   d. 120N

21. A parrot of mass 300g decides to rest on block C. What happens to the tension in the string between the ceiling and block A?
   a. It increases by 100N
   b. It increases by 300N
   c. It increases by 1N
   d. It increases by 3N

22. The string used to make the hanging toy will break if the tension in it exceeds 150N. How many similar parrots can the toy hold?
    a. Only 1
    b. 10 parrots, and they may choose to rest on any block they wish
    c. 10 parrots, but they must all rest only on block C
    d. 10 parrots, but they cannot move

23. A block is moving at a constant velocity of 50ms⁻¹ on a frictionless surface. Neglecting the effects of air resistance, what will cause a change in its movement?
    a. If it were made of a rougher material
    b. It its mass increased
    c. If it were pushed
    d. If it had a more streamlined shape

24. Which statement about the following forces is true?

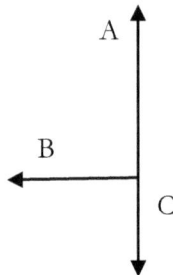

    a. The resultant force will be in the opposite direction of B
    b. The resultant force will lie between A and B
    c. The resultant force will lie between A and C
    d. It is impossible to know the direction of the resultant force

25. Two loads hang on a frictionless pulley. The strings have negligible mass. B has twice the mass of A. Take the mass of A to be 10kg. Choose the most accurate statement.

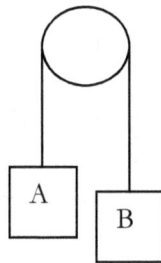

    a.   The tension in the string is (100+200)N
    b.   The tension in the string is (100-200)N
    c.   The tension in the string is (200-100)N
    d.   The tension in the string is 0N because the forces cancel each other out

26. A pendulum bob of 5 kg is suspended as shown below. Find the magnitude of the horizontal force holding it in place.

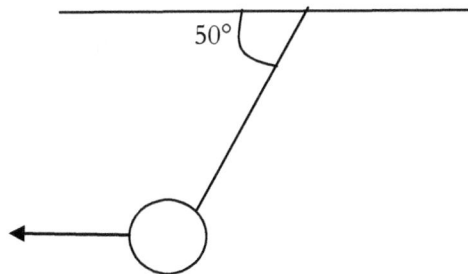

    a.   50.2N
    b.   59.5N
    c.   60.8N
    d.   63.3N

27. A signboard of mass 3kg hangs from two wires of equal length as shown below

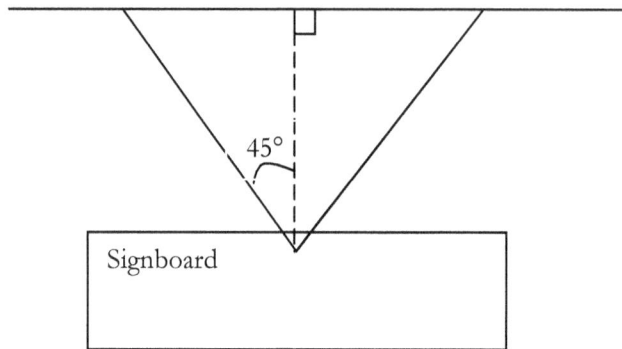

45°

Signboard

Find the tension in each wire.
   a.   1.06 N
   b.   2.12 N
   c.   3.18 N
   d.   4.24N

28. If each wire can only withstand a tension of 12N before it breaks, what is the maximum mass that the signboard can have?
   a.   4.24 N
   b.   8.48 N
   c.   12.72 N
   d.   16 97 N

29. A toy train with similar carriages is being pulled by a child with a constant velocity of 10m/s as shown below. The tension between the child's hand and the first carriage is 10N. what is the tension of the string between carriages B and C? Assume negligible friction.

| A | — | B | — | C | — | D | — | E | — 10N → |

    a.   0N
    b.   10N
    c.   8N
    d.   4N

30. The child pulls the toy train in question 1 onto a carpeted floor. The train now experiences a frictional force of 8N. What is the tension between the child's hand and carriage E if there is no change in the movement of the train?
    a.   2N
    b.   10N
    c.   0N
    d.   18N

31. Continuing from the question above, what is the new tension between carriages B and C?
    a.   0N
    b.   4N
    c.   7.2N
    d.   18N

32. The train is now back on the frictionless floor. The child wants to add more carriages. If the maximum force the child's body is able to exert is 18N, how many more carriages can he add, and still maintain the movement of the train?

    a. 2
    b. 4
    c. 8
    d. 9

33. Which statement about the resulting force of the following forces is true?

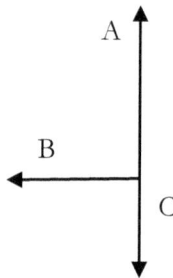

    a. The magnitude is the sum of the magnitudes of forces A, B and C
    b. It will require a force pointing to the north-west direction for equilibrium
    c. It will never be zero
    d. It will lie between B and C

34. Two loads hang on a frictionless pulley. A has a larger mass than B. The string has a negligible mass. What happens?

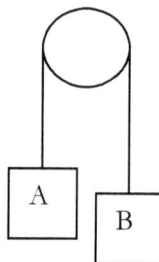

    a. A moves down with a constant velocity
    b. B moves up with constant velocity
    c. B moves up with decreasing velocity
    d. A moves down with increasing velocity

35. A moving car experiences a frictional force of 100N. Its velocity varies with time as shown below. Choose the most accurate statement about the forward driving force.

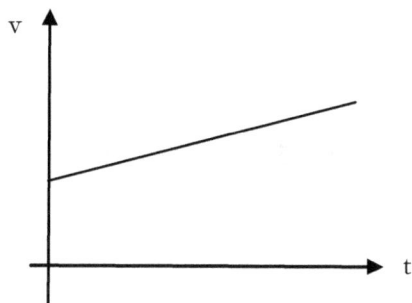

    a. It is zero
    b. It is constant at 100N
    c. It is constant at more than 100N
    d. It is increasing

36. A, B and C are non-zero forces acting on a stationary object. All of them act in different directions. Both A and C are perpendicular to B. Does the object start to move?
    a. Yes, because there will surely be a resultant force
    b. Yes, because as long as there is a force acting on an object, it must move
    c. No, because the forces cancel each other out
    d. Cannot be sure, because the forces might or might not cancel each other out

37. A motorcyclist is traveling at constant velocity of 50 km h^{-1}. The frictional force that the road exerts on each wheel is 100N. The motorcyclist and the motorcycle have a combined mass of 120kg. What is the forward force provided by the engine?
    a. 100 N
    b. 120 N
    c. 400 N
    d. 1200 N

38. The motorcyclist above suddenly realizes he is late for an appointment. He accelerates such that the engine's force now increases by 30%. What is his acceleration?
    a. 1.2 m/s^2
    b. 2.4 m/s^2
    c. 4.3 m/s^2
    d. 8.5 m/s^2

39. The motorcyclist above accelerates for 5 seconds before he starts moving with a constant velocity. Find this velocity.
    a. 21.65 m/s
    b. 51.65 m/s
    c. $71\ 65 \text{ m/s}$
    d. 81.65 m/s

40. Although the motorcyclist above is now moving at constant velocity, the force of the engine as well as the frictional force remain unchanged. Do you agree with this statement?
    a. Yes. The new engine force decreases until it is equal to the original frictional force.
    b. No. The frictional force increases until it is equal to the new engine force.
    c. Yes. Everything must always go back to their original states.
    d. No. The size of the forces are the same, but the directions change.

41. Three men start to pull a stationary rock as shown below. All three men are equidistant from each other and exert the same amount of force on the rock.

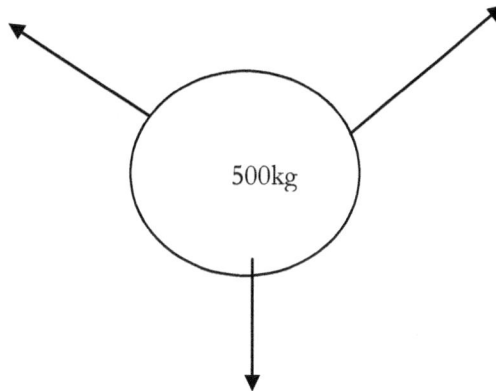

500kg

What happens to the rock?
- a. It does not move
- b. It moves up
- c. It moves down
- d. It moves sideways

42. A rock of 60kg moves from rest with a steadily increasing velocity. After 5s, it is moving at a velocity of 10m/s. What is the force exerted on the rock by each man?
- a. 50 N
- b. 60 N
- c. 120 N
- d. 600 N

43. Which is not a key assumption made in the previous question?
- a. There is no frictional force acting on the rock
- b. There is no air resistance acting on the rock
- c. The rock is on earth
- d. There is no human error in measuring the timing of 5 s

44. Why does it take a longer distance for a car to stop on a road covered with spilt oil than on a normal road?
    a. There is more friction, so the resultant force acting on the car is smaller
    b. There is more friction, so the resultant force acting on the car is larger
    c. There is less friction, so the resultant force acting on the car is smaller
    d. There is less friction, so the resultant force acting on the car is larger

45. This is a wheel of a lorry moving in the direction of the arrow. Which statement is true?

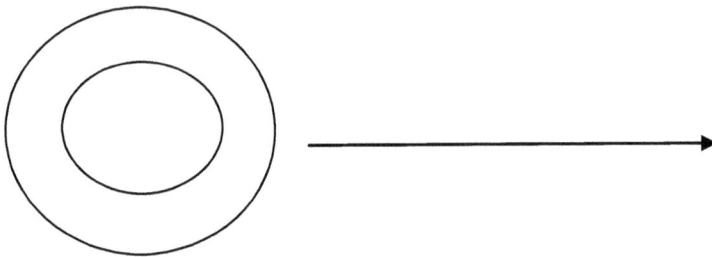

    a. The air resistance and the friction are both acting towards the right
    b. The air resistance and the friction are both acting towards the left
    c. The air resistance is acting towards the right and the friction is acting towards the left
    d. The air resistance is acting towards the left and the friction is acting towards the right

4 Moments [__ / 20]

1. Which statement is not true?
    a. Clockwise moment and anti-clockwise moment acting on an object must always cancel out
    b. Moment = magnitude of force x perpendicular distance from line of force to pivot
    c. Resultant moment of forces acting on an object must be zero
    d. Moment is a scalar quantity

2. Two boxes lie on opposite sides of an unbalanced see-saw as shown below. How should box B be moved, in order to balance the see-saw?

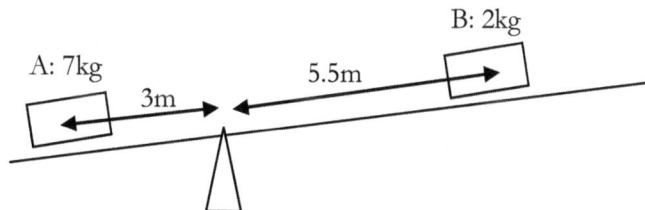

    1. 2.5m to the left
    2. 5m to the left
    3. 5m to the right
    4. 2.5m to the right

3. Why does a tightrope walker carry a long pole when performing?
    a. To look more impressive
    b. To keep his centre of gravity vertically above the rope
    c. To increase his mass to that the rope is more taut
    d. To spread his weight out evenly

4. A metre rule of weight 100g is pinned on a wall such that it is allowed to swing freely. The pin is at the 40cm mark. A weight of 500g is hung at the 0cm mark. What is the resultant moment about the pivot?
    a. 1.9 Nm clockwise
    b. 1.9 Nm anticlockwise
    c. 19 Nm clockwise
    d. 19 Nm anticlockwise

5. A uniform plank of mass 5kg lies on a pivot. It is 10m long. Where should a block of 10kg be placed on it such that the plank now lies parallel to the ground?

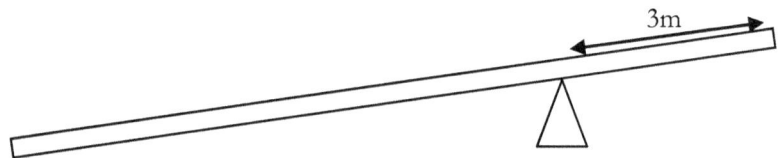

    a. 1m from the right of the plank
    b. 2m to the right of the pivot
    c. 8m from the left of the plank
    d. 3m to the left of the pivot

6. How does a balancing toy work?
    a. The center of gravity is above the pivot
    b. The center of gravity is below the pivot
    c. The base area is large
    d. The base area is small

7. There is a door fixed to a wall by two hinges.

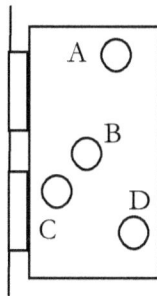

Which door knob will require the least force to open the door?
a. B
b. D
c. A
d. C

8. Explain the logic behind the answer to the previous question.
a. It is the nearest to the ground
b. It is the furthest from the ground
c. It is the furthest away from the pivot
d. It is the nearest to the pivot

9. A wheelbarrow carries an object. The combined weight of the object and the wheelbarrow is 500N, and it acts at the centre of the wheelbarrow. What is the minimum upward force required at the handles needed to support this weight?
a. 125N
b. 250N
c. 500N
d. 1000N

10. As a cyclist pedals, the positions of the pedals change as shown in diagrams A, B and C. The force that he applies on the pedals is constant throughout his journey.

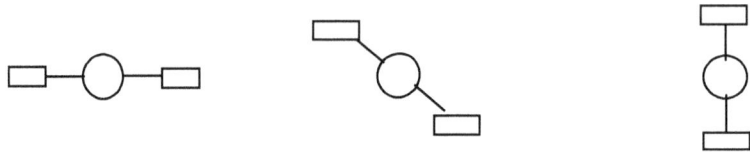

At which position is the cyclist exerting the largest moment about the pivot?
a. The one on the left
b. The one in the center
c. The one on the right
d. It is the same for all positions

11. Explain the logic behind the previous question.
a. The line of force is the nearest to the ground
b. The line of force is the furthest from the ground
c. The line of force is the furthest away from the pivot
d. The line of force is the nearest to the pivot

12. At which position is he exerting the smallest moment about the pivot?
a. The one on the right, because the moment is zero
b. The one on the left, because the moment is zero
c. The one in the center
d. It is the same for all positions

13. Which object is the most stable?

	Base area	Center of gravity
a.	Large	High
b.	Large	Low
c.	Small	High
d	Small	Low

14. Which statement is true?

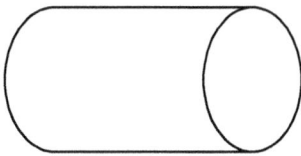

    a.   The object is in stable equilibrium
    b.   The object is in unstable equilibrium
    c.   The object is in neutral equilibrium
    d.   It cannot be determined what type of equilibrium the object is in

15. Where could the center of gravity of this object possibly be?

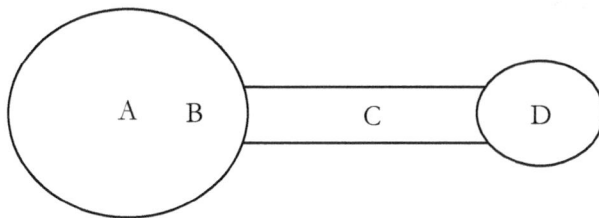

    a. B
    b. A
    c. D
    d. C

16. A 5N weight is placed at a position 1m from the right side of the plank. The plank now lies parallel to the ground. What is the mass of the uniform 10m long plank?

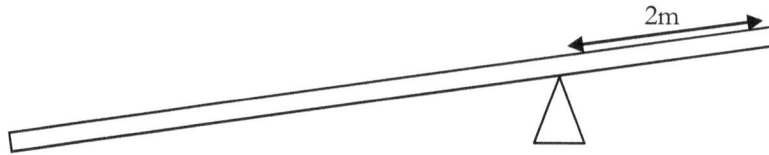

2m

    a.   1.67 N
    b.   2. 00 N
    c.   16.7 kg
    d.   20.00 kg

17. A 1kg weight placed at 0.5m from the right side of the 2kg plank causes it to become parallel to the ground. How far is the centre of gravity from the left side of the plank?

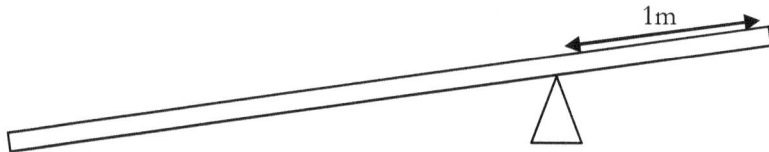

1m

    a.   4 m
    b.   5 m
    c.   6 m
    d.   1 m

18. Which statement is true for an object to be at equilibrium?
    a. Forces acting on the object must always be at opposite sides of the pivot
    b. Forces acting on the object must always be at the same side of the pivot
    c. Forces acting on the object can be on any side of the pivot
    d. There must be no forces acting on the object

19. What is the center of gravity of an object?
    a. The point at which all its mass seems to act
    b. The point at which all its mass acts
    c. The point at which all its weight seems to act
    d. The point at which all its weight acts

20. Which is not needed to find the center of gravity of a lamina?
    a. The mass of the lamina
    b. Letting the lamina hang freely
    c. Dropping a plumbline in front of the lamina and tracing out the line
    d. An intersection between traced plumblines

5 Work, energy, power [__ / 45]

1. A boy of mass 30kg runs up a flight of stairs in 30 seconds. What is the power of his body?

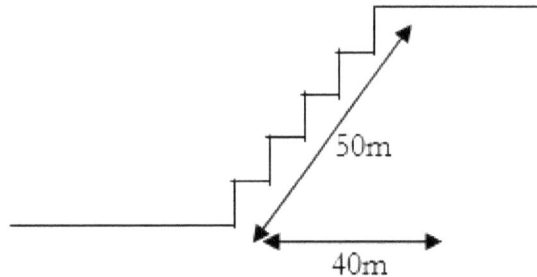

       a.   10W
       b.   30W
       c.   100W
       d.   300W

2. A sumo wrestler of mass 200kg pushes a wall with a force of 1500N. The wall crumbles. What is the work done by the sumo wrestler?
    a. 0 J
    b. 2000 J
    c. 1500 J
    d. 300 kJ

3. A ball falls from a height of 10m. At every bounce, 50% of the ball's energy is converted into heat and sound energy. What is the height that the ball bounces to after the 3rd bounce? Neglect air resistance.
    a. 1.0m
    b. 1.25m
    c. 2.50m
    d. 5.0m

4. A block is pushed at a constant velocity of 4ms^{-1}. The work done in moving it 5m is 100J. What is the frictional force acting on it?
   a. 0N
   b. 20N
   c. 50N
   d. 100N

5. Choose the most accurate statement.
   a. Kinetic energy is always converted to gravitational potential energy
   b. Energy is created through photosynthesis
   c. Work done by a car moving up a slope is only in overcoming friction
   d. Kinetic energy is zero when an object is not moving

6. A block of wood of mass 10kg is pulled up a ramp at a constant velocity of 2.0ms^{-1}. It experiences a frictional force of 5N.

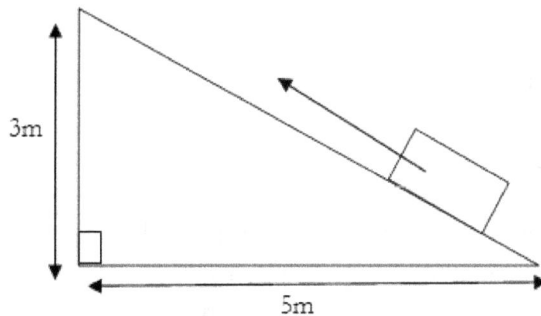

3m

5m

Find the work done by the pulling force.
   a. 15 Nm
   b. 25 Nm
   c. 29 Nm
   d. 50 Nm

7. It took 5s to pull the block up the ramp (refer to diagram above). What is the power of the pulling force?
   a. 3 W
   b. 5 W
   c. 5.8 W
   d. 10 W

8. A force of 100N is applied to a stationary block. It moves, experiencing an opposing frictional force of 20N. It covers a distance of 4m. Given that the force was exerted by a machine of power 100W, how long did the block take to move the entire 4m?
   a. 0.8 s
   b. 3.2 s
   c. 4.0 s
   d. 10 s

9. In the previous question, what was the amount of energy used to overcome friction?
   a. 40 J
   b. 80 J
   c. 400 J
   d. 800 J

10. A mass of water takes 0.5 hours to boil. How much heat energy is needed to boil the water using a 2000W kettle?
   a. 1 000 J
   b. 10 000 J
   c. 60 000 J
   d. 3 600 000 J

11. The heat energy used turns out to be 4,000kJ. Why do the numbers not tally?
   a. More energy is required as some energy is lost to the surroundings
   b. More energy is required as some energy is gained from the surroundings
   c. Less energy is required as some energy is lost to the surroundings
   d. More energy is required as some energy is gained from the surroundings

12. A block of mass 50kg is dropped from a building 500m tall and makes a dent in the ground that is 5cm deep. What is the speed at which it hits the ground?
   a. 71 m/s
   b. 100 m/s
   c. 158 m/s
   d. 187 m/s

13. What is the force that it exerts on the ground when it lands?
    a. 2 500 N
    b. 5 000 N
    c. 25 kN
    d. 5 000 kN

14. A ball with an initial velocity of 5ms^{-1} rolls across a surface and eventually comes to a rest after 10m. It experiences 6N of frictional force throughout its motion. What is the weight of the stone?
    a. 4.8 kg
    b. 48 kg
    c. 4.8 N
    d. 48 N

15. A stone rolling off a cliff has
    a. Only gravitational potential energy
    b. Only kinetic energy
    c. Both gravitational potential energy and kinetic energy
    d. Neither gravitational potential energy not kinetic energy

16. The efficiency of a car's 2000kW engine is 70%. It is used for 10 minutes to drive at a constant velocity against a frictional force of 100kN. How far does it travel?
    a. 8.4 km
    b. 84 km
    c. 840 km
    d. 8400 km

17. A pendulum starts at A. It swings back and forth. At which point does it have the most KE / GPE? Ignore air resistance.

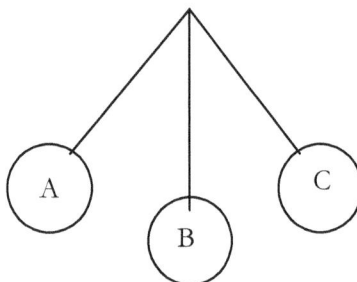

	KE	GPE
a.	A	C
b.	A,C	B
c.	B	A,C
d.	A,B,C	A,B,C

18. A rock falls freely to the ground from rest, from a height of 5m. When it is 2m above the ground, what is the ratio of its kinetic energy to its gravitational potential energy?
     a.   1:1
     b.   3:2
     c.   2:3
     d.   1:0

19. What is power?
     a.   The total energy used in completing a task
     b.   Authority
     c.   Energy exerted each second
     d.   Work done

20. As a man runs a marathon, the pressure exerted on him by the wind is 100Pa. Given that the surface area of his body in contact with the wind is 200m², what is the minimum force that his body has to exert to overcome the wind?
    a. 20 N
    b. 500 N
    c. 20 000 N
    d. 500 000 N

21. Continuing from the question above, the marathon is 42.5km long. What is the man's total work done against the wind?
    a. 2125 J
    b. 850 kJ
    c. 212 500 J
    d. 850 000 kJ

22. Continuing from the question above, if the man took 3.5 hours to complete the marathon, what is the power of his body?
    a. 1 687 W
    b. 6 746 W
    c. 67 460 W
    d. 168 700 W

23. A road for vehicles that leads to the peak of a steep mountain winds around the mountain instead of making a beeline from the bottom to the top. Why?
    a. Vehicles can save fuel because a winding road uses less energy
    b. Vehicles need more time to reach the top, decreasing the power needed
    c. It prevents the vehicles from falling off the mountain
    d. It is more efficient because more power can be used

24. A car of mass 500kg moves up a slope and then down the other side. What is the minimum power needed by the car in order to reach the peak of the 300m high slope in 10 minutes?

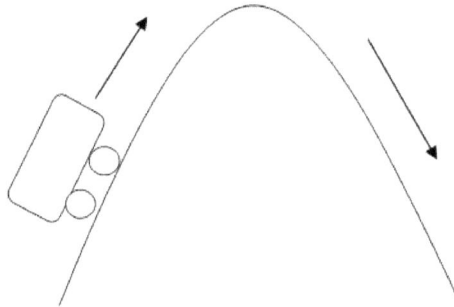

      a.   1 500 W
      b.   2 500 W
      c.   5 000 W
      d.   150 000 W

25. Continuing from the question above, halfway down the slope, its velocity is 50 km h^{-1}. What is its total energy at this point?
      a.   24 kJ
      b.   40 kJ
      c.   750 kJ
      d.   1 500 kJ

26. Continuing from the question above, it reaches the bottom of the slope with a velocity of 75 km h^{-1}. What was the work done by the car against air resistance and friction?
      a.   12 500 J
      b.   93 750 J
      c.   156 250 J
      d.   1 406 250 J

27. A stone of weight 5N is thrown vertically upwards from ground level. What is the work done against gravity of the stone at the point at which it has travelled 5m upwards?

——————————

    a.   0 J
    b. 10 J
    c.   25 J
    d. 125 J

28. Continuing from the question above, what is the gravitational potential energy of the stone at that same point?
    a.   0 J
    b. 10 J
    c.   25 J
    d. 125 J

29. Continuing from the question above, what is the kinetic energy of the stone when it reaches its maximum height?
    a.   0 J
    b. 10 J
    c.   25 J
    d. 125 J

30. A man weighing 500N runs up a vertical flight of stairs. He reaches the top in 2 hours and finds himself 5km above ground level. How much energy is burnt by his body?

    a. 347 J
    b. 20 833 J
    c. 1 250 kJ
    d. 2 500 kJ

31. Continuing from the question above, what is the power of his body?

    a. 347 W
    b. 20 833 W
    c. 1 250 kW
    d. 2 500 kW

32. Continuing from the question above, another man climbs up a winding flight of stairs to the same height. He takes 5 hours. How much energy is burnt by his body?

    a. 416 J
    b. 500 J
    c. 2 500 kJ
    d. 5 208 kJ

33. Continuing from the question above, what is the power of his body?

    a. 139 W
    b. 347 W
    c. 3125 W
    d. 4250 W

34. A car has a power of 5000W. It exerts a constant force of 200N on a block it is pulling. What is the speed at which the block moves?

    a. $10ms^{-1}$
    b. $25ms^{-1}$
    c. $100ms^{-1}$
    d. $250ms^{-1}$

35. What happens to a man's gravitational potential energy when he falls off a cliff?
    a. It is converted into sound energy as he screams
    b. It is converted into kinetic energy
    c. It is converted into kinetic energy and more gravitational potential energy
    d. It is converted into more gravitational potential energy

36. A crane lifts a crate up. Which path should it take such that is least work is needed to be done?
    a. 10° to the ground
    b. 45° to the ground
    c. Perpendicular to the ground
    d. Parallel to the ground

37. When a truck is driven up a mountain with a net forward force of 2000N acting on it, what happens?
    a. It loses gravitational potential energy and kinetic energy
    b. It loses gravitational potential energy but gains kinetic energy
    c. It gains gravitational potential energy but loses kinetic energy
    d. It gains gravitational potential energy and kinetic energy

38. A block with a constant velocity of 9ms⁻¹ moves from a horizontal, frictionless surface up a frictionless ramp.

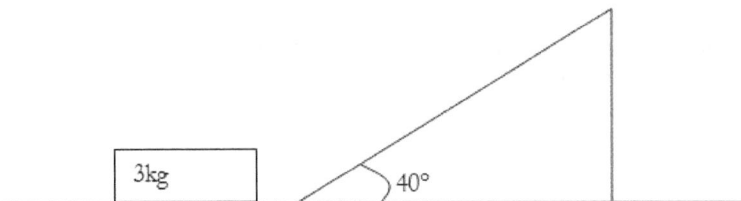

What is the maximum height it will reach?

    a. 3.00 m
    b. 4.05 m
    c. 4.50 m
    d. 9.00 m

39. Continuing from the question above, if instead, it experiences a frictional force of 6N when moving up the ramp, what will be its maximum height?
    a.   1.96 m
    b.   3.08 m
    c.   5. 04 m
    d.   7.02 m

40. Continuing from the question above, if the ramp had been half as steep, how much higher would the block have been able to move?
    a.   Half the height
    b.   The same height
    c.   Twice the height
    d.   4 times the height

41. A ball at point A is rolling to the right at a speed of 15ms^{-1}.

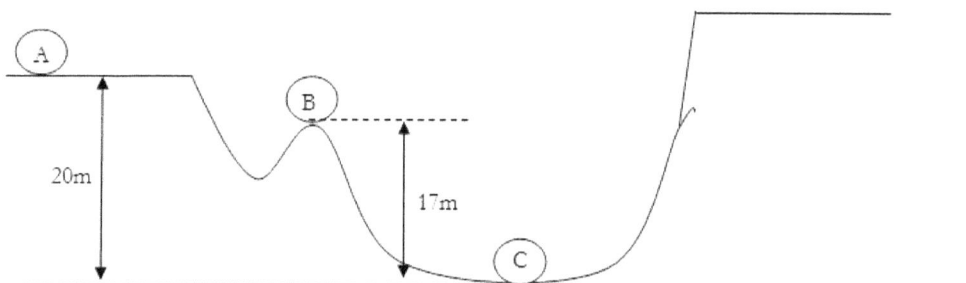

    What form(s) of energy does the ball have at point A?

    1.   Gravitational potential energy only
    2.   Kinetic energy only
    3.   Both gravitational potential energy and kinetic energy
    4.   Neither gravitational potential energy nor kinetic energy

42. Continuing from the question above, what is the ball's speed at point B?
    a.   13.1 m/s
    b.   15.0 m/s
    c.   16.9 m/s
    d.   17.2 m/s

43. Continuing from the question above, what is the balls gravitational potential energy at point C?
    a. 0.0 J
    b. 7.5 J
    c. 15.0 J
    d. 112.5 J

44. Continuing from the question above, w here is the final position of the ball?
    a. The valley between position A and position B
    b. Position B
    c. Position C
    d. On top of the cliff, on the right hand side of C

45. Explain the logic behind the answer to the previous question.
    a. The ball must roll backwards
    b. The ball cannot gain energy from the surroundings
    c. The ball must stay at the lowest point
    d. The ball's final height must be between the floor and its original height

6 Pressure [__ / 40]

1. What must the minimum water pressure in a pipe at ground level be in order to pump water up a building 800 m high? [Density of water = 1000 kg m^{-3}]
   a. 8×10^3
   b. 8×10^4
   c. 8×10^5
   d. 8×10^6

2. A mountain climber brings a barometer up a mountain with him. What does he observe about the mercury level?
   a. It is lower than when he was at ground level, because the pressure has increased
   b. It is lower than when he was at ground level, because the pressure has decreased
   c. It is higher than when he was at ground level, because the pressure has increased
   d. It is higher than when he was at ground level, because the pressure has decreased

3. Which graph shows the correct relationship between pressure and volume?

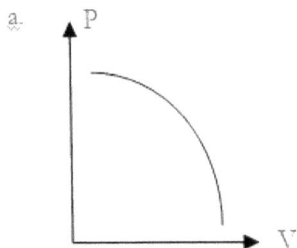

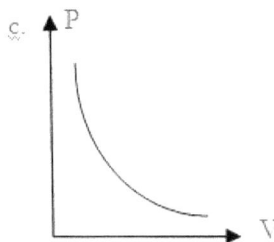

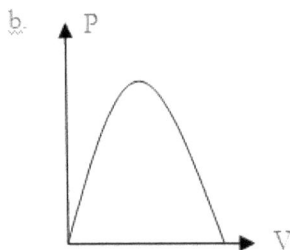

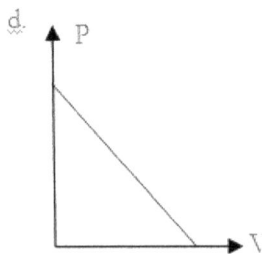

4. Two solid cubes made of the same material are placed side by side. The length of each side of the second cube is three times the length of each side of the first cube. Which of the following statements is correct?
   a. Both cubes exert equal pressure on the ground
   b. The second cube exerts twice the pressure that the first cube exerts on the ground
   c. The second cube exerts four times the pressure that the first cube exerts on the ground
   d. The second cube exerts eight times the pressure that the first cube exerts on the ground

5. As a bubble rises from the bottom of the sea to the top, what happens to the air inside it?
   a. Both the density and the pressure increase
   b. Both the density and the pressure decrease
   c. The density increases and the pressure decreases
   d. The density decreases and the pressure increases

6. The pressure at a point at the bottom of a bottle of coke does not depend on
   a. The density of the coke
   b. The level of coke in the bottle
   c. Gravity
   d. The radius of the bottle

7. A mercury barometer has its radius multiplied by 4. What happens to the height of the mercury column?
   a. It halves
   b. It does not change
   c. It doubles
   d. It is also multiplied by 4 times

8. Which graph shows the correct relationship between pressure and temperature (in Kelvin)?

a.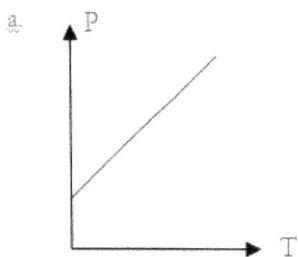

c.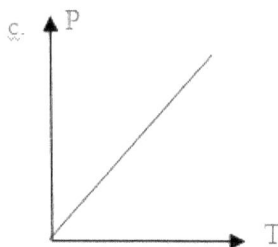

b.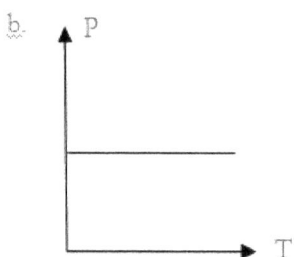

d.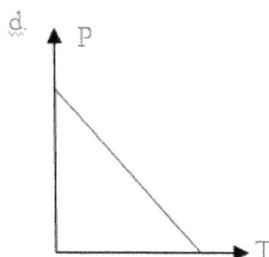

9. The pressure of a volume of air held in a syringe is X Pa. If the piston is pushed such that the volume of air is halved, what happens to the pressure?
    a. Remains constant
    b. ½ X
    c. X
    d. 2X

10. The pressure of a gas in a sealed container at a temperature of 30°C is measured as Y Pa. The container is cooled/heated such that the pressure of the gas is now 3Y. What is the final temperature of the gas?
    a. 10°C
    b. 30°C
    c. 90°C
    d. 120°C

11. When a volume of gas is compressed, why does the pressure increase?
    a. The gas molecules shrink
    b. The frequency of the gas molecules colliding with the walls of the container increases
    c. The gas molecules expand
    d. The spaces in between the molecules decrease

12. Which statement is true?
    a. The product of pressure and volume is always a constant
    b. The product of pressure and volume is a constant only when temperature is kept constant
    c. Temperature is inversely proportional to pressure
    d. Volume is directly proportional to pressure

13. A U-shaped tube holds water and liquid X of height 6 cm. The density of water is 1000 kg m^{-3} and the acceleration due to gravity is 10 m s^{-2}.

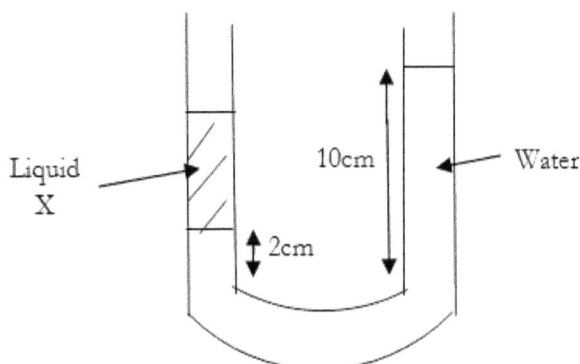

Is liquid X denser or less dense than water? Explain why you think so.

    a. Denser. The height of the liquid and its density must move in opposite directions.
    b. Denser. Water is the least dense liquid that exists.
    c. Less dense. The height of the liquid and its density must move in the same direction.
    d. Less dense. Water is the most dense liquid that exists.

14. Calculate the density of liquid X, given that the height of liquid X is 6cm.
    a. 600 kg m^{-3}
    b. 800 kg m^{-3}
    c. 1 333 kg m^{-3}
    d. 6 000 kg m^{-3}

15. A lady wearing stilettos walks into a clump of mud. Her heels sink into the mud. Why?
    a. The pressure exerted by her heels increased
    b. The surface area of her heels in contact with the ground decreased
    c. Mud is soft
    d. The force exerted by her body increased

16. An alien has a mass of 20 kg. Acceleration due to the gravitational force of his planet is 5 ms^{-1}. He has five feet of surface areas 1 m^2, 2 m^2, 3 m^2, 4 m^2 and 5 m^2. What is the pressure exerted on the ground by its foot of surface area 5 m^2?
    a. 4 Pa
    b. 5 Pa
    c. 25 Pa
    d. 100 Pa

17. There is trapped air in a capillary tube held by a 10 cm long column of mercury. Atmospheric pressure is 76 cm Hg. What is the pressure of the trapped air when the tube is held parallel to the ground?
    a. 66 cm Hg
    b. 76 cm Hg
    c. 86 cm Hg
    d. 760 cm Hg

18. The tank contains water. The cross sectional area of the water column on the left is 3 cm^2 and the cross sectional area of the water column on the right is 9 cm^2. Take the density of the water to be 1000 kg m^{-3}.

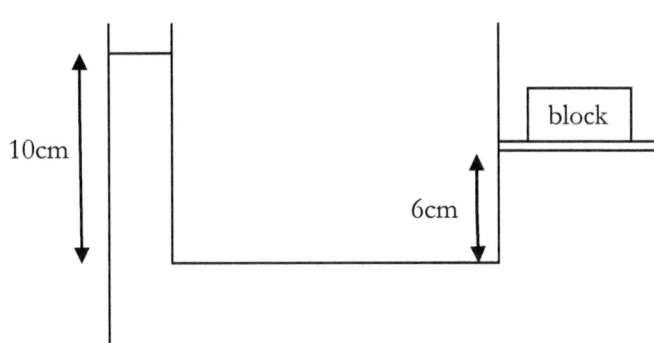

Calculate the weight of the block.

       a. 0.0003 N

       b. 0.0036 N

       c. 3.6 N

       d. 9 N

19. Another block can be placed on the surface of the water at the left-hand limb to make the water levels at both limbs equal. If the weight of the first block is 6N, what must the mass of this second block be?

       a.   2 N

       b.   20 g

       c.   18 N

       d.   20 kg

20. Which graph show the correct relationship between pressure and volume?

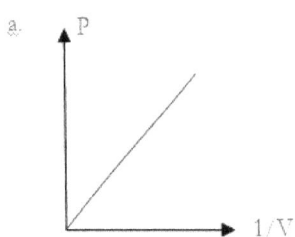

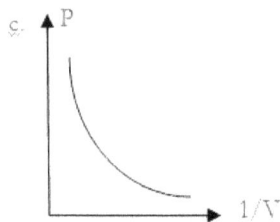

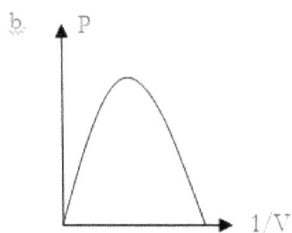

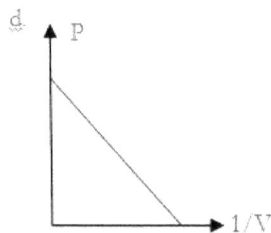

21. A narrow capillary tube with one side open is held inverted with the closed side on the top. There is a column of trapped air held by a mercury plug of length 7cm. What is the pressure of the trapped air? [Atmospheric pressure = 76 cm Hg]
    a. 69 cm Hg
    b. 76 cm Hg
    c. 83 cm Hg
    d. 100 cm Hg

22. The liquids in barometers A and B are different. They are placed side by side. Which of the following statements could explain the observation?

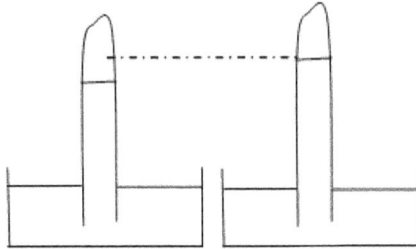

    a.   Liquid B is less dense than liquid A
    b.   Liquid B is denser than liquid A
    c.   Liquids A and B have the same density
    d.   There is less atmospheric pressure acting on barometer B

23. The barometers below are placed side by side. Which one is recording the highest atmospheric pressure?

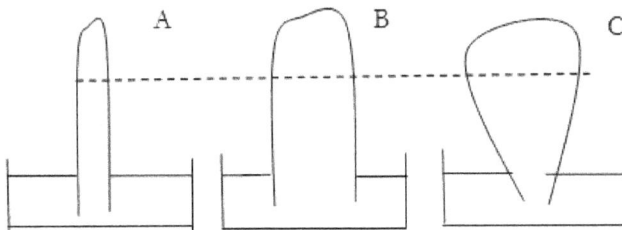

    a.   Barometer A
    b.   Barometer B
    c.   Barometer C
    d.   None of the above

24. Which shows the reading of the atmospheric pressure?

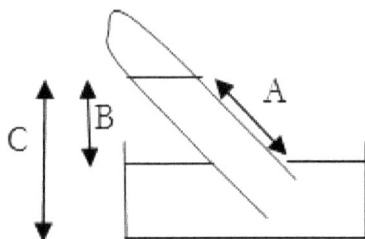

    a. B
    b. C
    c. A
    d. None of the above. This barometer cannot show an accurate reading.

25. The pressure of a volume of air held in a syringe is X Pa. If the piston is pushed such that the volume of air is reduced by 30%, what happens to the pressure?
    a. 0.7X Pa
    b. 1.3X Pa
    c. X Pa
    d. 1.43X Pa

26. A mercury barometer has a column of mercury 76mm tall. Somebody accidentally knocks it. The column is pushed such that it now lies at an angle of 45° to the ground. What happens to the height of the mercury?
    a. It increases
    b. It decreases
    c. It remains the same
    d. It is not possible to tell

27. The barometer is now carried up mount everest. What happens to the mercury level? Explain.
    a. It remains the same because mercury barometers have a constant height
    b. It decreases because the pressure has decreased
    c. It increases because the pressure has increased
    d. The decreases because the pressure has increased

28. A syringe holds 100cm³ of gaseous element X at a pressure P. The piston of the syringe is pushed such that the volume decreases by 80%. Find the new pressure of the gas in terms of P.
    a. 0.2 P
    b. 0.8 P
    c. 5 P
    d. 12.5 P

29. The piston is shifted back to its original position. The gas is then pumped directly into another syringe that has 3 times the cross-sectional area of the first syringe. The length of the gaseous column remains the same. Find the new pressure of the gas in terms of P.
    a. 1/9 P
    b. 1/3 P
    c. 3 P
    d. 9 P

30. The gas is now pushed back to the original syringe and resumes the original pressure P. The syringe is heated but the material of the syringe does not expand. The pressure remains at P. What is the new volume of the gas?
    a. Less than P
    b. P
    c. More than P
    d. Not enough information given

31. Barometer A contains liquid A and barometer B contains liquid B. Which of the following statements must be true?

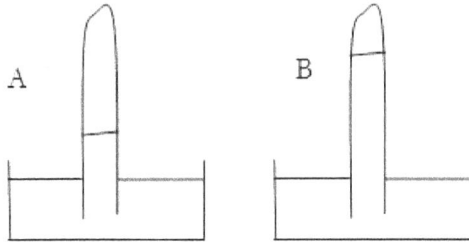

A   B

    a.   Liquid A is kept at a higher temperature than liquid B
    b.   Liquid B is kept at a higher temperature than liquid A
    c.   Liquid A has a higher density than liquid B
    d.   Liquid B has a higher density than liquid A

32. Four barometers are placed side by side. Which one is showing a wrong reading?

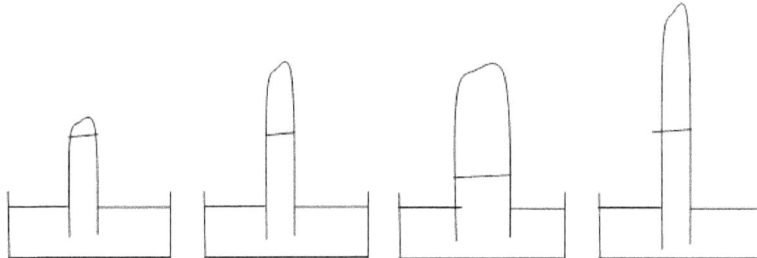

    a.   Barometer A, because the vacuum at the top is too small
    b.   Barometer C, because the liquid level should be higher
    c.   Barometer D, because the liquid level should be lower
    d.   Barometer D, because the liquid level should be higher

33. An air bubble of volume 2cm³ rises from the bottom of a tank to the surface. The pressure exerted by the water on the bubble at the bottom of the tank is twice that of the atmospheric pressure. What is the volume of the air bubble just before it bursts at the surface?

    a.   1 cm³

    b.   4 cm³

    c.   6 cm³

    d.   8 cm³

34. A gas at a pressure of X Pa in a sealed cube is transferred to another cube with a length that is 3 times that of the original. It is then heated such that the temperature of the gas is now 1/3 that of the original. What happens to the pressure of this gas?

    a.   No change

    b.   9 X

    c.   1/27 X

    d.   1/81 X

35. The liquids in barometers A and B are the same. They are found on planet A and planet B respectively. Which of the following statements is most likely to be true?

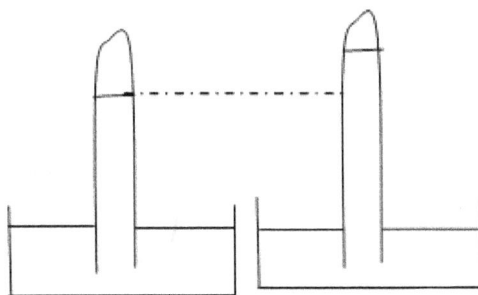

    a.   The atmospheric pressure of planet A is more than that of planet B

    b.   The density of the liquid in barometer B is lower than that in barometer A

    c.   Planet B has a higher temperature than planet A

    d.   A man exerting the same amount of energy jumps higher on planet B than on planet A

36. A four-legged animal has a mass of 6kg. Each leg has a surface area of 1cm² in contact with the ground. Calculate the pressure exerted by animal on the ground.
    a. 6 Pa
    b. 15 000 Pa
    c. 60 000 Pa
    d. 150 000 Pa

37. Calculate the pressure exerted on the ground by each foot of the animal.
    a. 6 Pa
    b. 15 000 Pa
    c. 60 000 Pa
    d. 150 000 Pa

38. If all its legs fused into 1 leg without changing the mass of the animal or its total surface area in contact with the ground, what would happen to the pressure exerted by the animal on the ground?
    a. Higher
    b. Lower
    c. Same
    d. Not enough information to make a conclusion

39. If the animal grew an additional leg instead, explain how it would affect the pressure exerted by the animal on the ground. Assume its mass remains the same.
    a. It will not change, because its mass is still the same
    b. It will increase, because the surface area increases
    c. It will decrease, because the surface area increases
    d. It will increase, because the surface area decreases

40. When a mercury barometer is heated, the mercury expands. What happens to its reading?
    a. It will become inaccurate as the height will increase
    b. It will become inaccurate as the height will decrease
    c. It will remain accurate as the height will not change
    d. It will remain accurate as the height will increase

7 Temperature and Heat [__ / 55]

1. Water is not used as a thermometric liquid because…
    a. It does not expand uniformly
    b. It has no colour
    c. It sticks to the side of the glass
    d. The range of temperature it can measure is too small

2. To make a thermometer more sensitive,
    a. Use thinner glass
    b. Use a smaller bore
    c. Use a larger bore
    d. Use a longer stem

3. A alcohol-in-glass thermometer is used to measure the temperature of liquid X. as liquid X is heated up, what happens to the alcohol?
    a. Its density remains constant
    b. Its density increases
    c. Its mass does not change
    d. Its mass increases

4. A liquid coolant should have…
    a. A high latent heat of fusion
    b. A low latent heat of fusion
    c. A high latent heat of vaporization
    d. A low latent heat of fusion

5. Two similar cups are filled up. One contains liquid P and the other contains liquid Q. The liquids are at thermal equilibrium. After standing for 10 minutes, the cup containing liquid Q feels significantly cooler. Why?
    a. Liquid Q has a higher specific heat capacity
    b. Liquid Q has a lower specific heat capacity
    c. Liquid Q has a higher latent heat of vaporization
    d. Liquid Q has a lower latent heat of vaporization

6. When a copper bar is placed under intense heat, what does not increase?
    a. Its volume
    b. Its surface area
    c. Its specific heat capacity
    d. Its internal energy

7. When air is pumped into a balloon at constant temperature, the pressure of the air inside the balloon increases because...
    a. The air molecules have more kinetic energy
    b. There are more air molecules hitting the skin of the balloon
    c. The air molecules expand
    d. The air molecules move faster

8. A dining table and a dining chair are made of the same type of wood. Which statement is true?
    a. Both have the same heat capacity
    b. The dining table has a higher specific heat capacity
    c. The dining chair has a lower specific heat capacity
    d. The dining chair has a lower latent heat of fusion

9. What will decrease the rate of a block of ice melting?
    a. Increasing the power of the heating element
    b. Increasing the surface area of the ice while keeping the mass constant
    c. Decreasing the power of the heating element
    d. Decreasing the surface area of the ice while keeping the mass constant

10. The latent heat of fusion of a substance is the amount of heat energy needed to..
    a. Change the temperature of 1kg of the substance by 1K
    b. Change 1kg of a substance from the liquid state to the gaseous state
    c. Increase the temperature of 1kg of the substance by 1K
    d. Change 1kg of a substance from the solid state to the liquid state

11. A beaker of water of 0.5kg at room temperature of 25°C is heated. How much heat is needed to increase its temperature to 100°C? Assume that the specific heat capacity of water is 4200 J °Kg^{-1} C^{-1}.
    a. 4 200 J
    b. 52 500 J
    c. 157 500 J
    d. 210 000 J

12. State an assumption used in your calculation above.
    a. The heat came from a Bunsen burner
    b. The water did not expand
    c. There was no heat transfer to the surroundings
    d. The water was in a glass beaker

13. 200 KJ of heat is supplied to a glass cup of 2 kg. Currently, the temperature of the cup is at 25°C. What will be the final temperature of the cup after heat is supplied to it? Assume specific heat capacity of glass is 670 J °Kg^{-1} C^{-1}.
    a. 127 °C
    b. 124 °C
    c. 149 °C
    d. 174 °C

14. A heater supplies 20W of power to a kettle containing water of mass 20 kg. How long must the heater be connected to the kettle to raise the temperature of the water from 20°C to 80°C? Assume that the specific heat capacity of water is 4200 J °Kg^{-1} C^{-1}.
    a. 4 200 seconds
    b. 70 hours
    c. 70 minutes
    d. 252 000 minutes

15. A block of ice at freezing point is heated until it melts and then boils. 17 000 J of heat is needed to melt the block of ice. Given that the specific latent heat of fusion of ice is 340 kJ kg^{-1}, find the mass of the block of ice.
    a. 0.05 kg
    b. 0.5 kg
    c. 5.78 kg
    d. 20 kg

16. How much heat is needed to fully boil this mass of water into water vapour? Assume that the specific latent heat of vaporization of ice is 2200 kJ kg^{-1}.
    a. 110 J
    b. 440 J
    c. 44 000 J
    d. 110 000 J

17. 110 000 J of heat is needed to fully melt a block of ice at freezing point into water. Given that the specific latent heat of fusion of water is 340 kJ kg^{-1}, find the mass of the block of ice.
    a. 309 g
    b. 324 g
    c. 3.09 kg
    d. 3.4 kg

18. The mass of the block of ice in the question above is found to be less than what you have calculated. What could not be a possible reason?
    a. Some of the energy was absorbed by the surrounding air
    b. Some of the energy was absorbed by the container
    c. The experiment was conducted in an enclosed place
    d. The energy transfer was not efficient

19. The heater used carries a rating of 200W. How long did it take to melt the ice?
    a. 220 hours
    b. 220 seconds
    c. 550 seconds
    d. 550 minutes

20. A vacuum flask is able to keep its contents warm for extended periods of time because
    a. It prevents heat transfer through conduction only
    b. It prevents heat transfer through convection only
    c. It prevents heat transfer through conduction and convection only
    d. It prevents heat transfer through conduction, convection and radiation

21. Which of the following mugs is most suitable for keeping coffee warm?

A	White	Shiny
B	Black	Shiny
C	White	Dull
D	Black	Dull

22. Which is the most probable reason for choosing to use a thermocouple over a mercury-in-glass thermometer?
    a. Thermocouples are cheaper
    b. Mercury is poisonous
    c. Thermocouples have larger ranges
    d. Mercury -in-glass thermometers can be difficult to read

23. Absolute zero occurs at...
    a. 0 °C
    b. 273 °C
    c. 273 K
    d. 273 K

24. A thermometer reads -3°C in pure melting ice and 97°C in pure boiling water. Substance X has a freezing point of 10°C and a boiling point of 30°C. What is the range of temperature at which substance X is a liquid, as measured by this thermometer?
    a. 17°C
    b. 20°C
    c. 23°C
    d. 40°C

25. When heat is supplied to equal masses of liquid X and liquid Y at room temperature, substance Y starts to boil sooner than substance X. What could explain this?

    I: Substance Y has a lower boiling point
    II: Substance X has a higher specific heat capacity
    III: Substance Y has a lower relative molecular mass

    a. II only
    b. I and II only
    c. II and III only
    d. I, III and III

26. The specific heat capacities of water, substance X and substance Y are 4200 J $°Kg^{-1} C^{-1}$, 2400 J $°Kg^{-1} C^{-1}$ and 420 J $°Kg^{-1} C^{-1}$ respectively. Equal masses of each are heated. Their temperatures are taken after 5 minutes. Which is the correct order of the readings, in order of increasing temperature?
    a. Water, X, Y
    b. Y, X, water
    c. All show the same reading
    d. X, Y, water

27. A heater with a power rating of 300W is used to fully melt 10g of crushed ice. Given that the specific latent heat of fusion of ice is 340 kJ kg^{-1} and the specific latent heat of vaporization of water is 2200 kJ kg^{-1}, find the heat lost to the surroundings if the process took 20 seconds.
    a. 2.6 J
    b. 260 J
    c. 2600 J
    d. 26 000 J

28. The graph shows how the temperature of a mass of substance X changes as it is heated. At the beginning of the experiment, substance X is a liquid. By the end of the experiment, it had become a gas. What can be inferred?

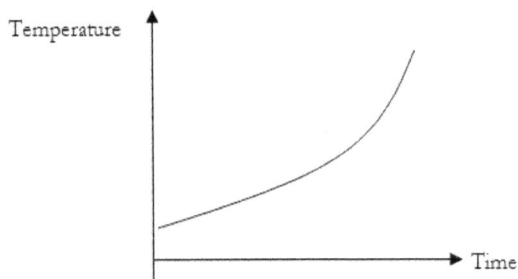

I: Substance X is not suitable to be used in thermometers
II: Substance X is not pure
III: The heat capacity of substance X varies inversely with its temperature

    a.   None of the statements are correct
    b.   Only statement I is correct
    c.   Only statement II is correct
    d.   Statements I, II and III are all correct

29. As a car moves, what happens to the air in its tires?
    a.   The air particles move faster
    b.   The volume of the air increases
    c.   The air particles expand
    d.   The air condenses into a liquid

30. A mass of water of 0.5kg is heated from -50°C to 150°C. State the melting and boiling points of the mass of water.
    a.   -50°C to 150°C respectively
    b.   0°C to 150°C respectively
    c.   -50°C to 100°C respectively
    d.   0°C to 100°C respectively

31. For the experiment in the previous question, a heater of power rating 200 kW was used. How long did the process take? The specific heat capacity of ice and water is 4200 J $^{\circ}$Kg^{-1} C^{-1}. The specific latent heat of fusion of ice is 340 kJ kg^{-1}. The specific latent heat of vaporization of water is 2200 kJ kg^{-1}.
    a. 0.29 hours
    b. 2.1 seconds
    c. 2.1 hours
    d. 3 370 seconds

32. 20 000 J of heat is supplied by a heater. It changes 10 kg of a substance from the solid state to the liquid state. What is the specific latent heat of fusion of this substance?
    a. 2 000 J/g
    b. 2 kJ/kg
    c. 476 J/kg
    d. Not enough information to determine

33. The same amount of heat as the question above also changes 10 kg of another substance from the liquid state to the gaseous state. What is the specific latent heat of vaporization of this substance?
    a. Same as the answer above
    b. Larger than the answer above
    c. Smaller than the answer above
    d. Not enough information to determine

34. A piece of wire has a resistance of 5.0Ω in melting substance X and 7.0Ω in boiling substance X. Substance X has a melting point of -20°C. At room temperature of 25°C, the resistance of the wire is 5.2Ω. Find the boiling point of substance X.
    a. 87 °C
    b. 100 °C
    c. 405 °C
    d. 430 °C

35. What assumption must be made about the resistance of the wire for your calculation to hold?
    a. It is very high
    b. It is very low
    c. It increases linearly with temperature
    d. It is a constant

36. A sheet of aluminium foil is shiny on one side and dull on the other side. It is used to line a barbeque grill. Which side should face the fire and which side should face the food? Explain.
    a. The dull side should face the fire as dull surfaces absorb heat through radiation very well
    b. The shiny side should face the fire as shiny surfaces absorb heat through radiation very well
    c. The dull side should face the food as dull surfaces absorb heat through radiation very well
    d. The shiny side should face the food as shiny surfaces absorb heat through radiation very well

37. This foil is also used to wrap food to keep them warm for late comers. Which side of the foil should face the food? Explain.
    a. The shiny side, as shiny surfaces absorb heat through radiation very poorly
    b. The shiny side, as shiny surfaces absorb heat through radiation very well
    c. The dull side, as dull surfaces absorb heat through radiation very well
    d. The dull side, as dull surfaces absorb heat through radiation very poorly

38. Will the foil work the same way in space? Explain.
    a. No, because there is no air
    b. Yes, because no medium is required for heat transfer through radiation
    c. No, because there is no light, and so there is no difference between shiny an dull surfaces
    d. Yes, because light is not required for radiation to take place

39. A solid is heated. What happens?

	Density	Reason
a.	Increases	Volume decreases while mass remains constant
b.	Increases	Mass increases while volume remains constant
c.	Decreases	Volume increases while mass remains constant
d.	Decreases	Mass decreases while volume remains constant

40. Convectional current movement is an important factor to consider when designing…
    a. Bunsen burners
    b. Refrigerators
    c. Balloons
    d. Roofs

41. Fibre is used to insulate homes in temperate countries because…
    a. It gives out heat when the surrounding temperature drops
    b. It reflects heat energy
    c. It traps air
    d. It is a poor conductor of heat

42. People living on mountain tops cook their eggs much faster than people living in coastal areas. Why?
    a. The increased pressure increases the boiling point of water
    b. The increased pressure decreases the boiling point of water
    c. The decreased pressure decreases the boiling point of water
    d. The decreased pressure increases the boiling point of water

43. 4 similar bars made of different metals are heated. The following information is gathered. Which is the best conductor of heat?

Metal	Initial temperature	Final temperature	Time taken
A	10°C	20°C	15s
B	20°C	30°C	10s
C	10°C	50°C	30s
D	20°C	100°C	80s

    a.   D
    b.   C
    c.   B
    d.   All of them are equally good conductors because they are all metals

44. A body of liquid is heated from 20°C to 50°C. What is the temperature change in Kelvin?
    a.   273 K
    b.   (50-20) K
    c.   273 x (50-20)K
    d.   273 + (50-20)K

45. The boiling point of pure water is…
    a.   0°C
    b.   273 °C
    c.   273 K
    d.   373 K

46. Why do the junctions of thermocouples have low heat capacities?
    a. Materials with high heat capacities are dangerous
    b. So that they respond quickly to temperature changes
    c. So that they do not melt under high temperatures
    d. Materials with low heat capacities react uniformly with temperature changes

47. A house catches fire. An aerosol can of paint left on the shelf explodes. Why?
    a. The gas molecules in the can move faster
    b. The liquid paint in the can expands and bursts out
    c. Aerosol cans are made of a special type of flammable metal
    d. The fire causes the can to expand too rapidly

48. Which of the following is not true about radiation?
    a. It can happen in spaced
    b. The colour of an object influences its ability to transfer heat through radiation
    c. The higher the temperature, the more efficient the radiation
    d. An object with a smooth surface will take a longer time to heat up through radiation

49. Radiation consists of...
    a. Brownian particles
    b. Infra-red waves
    c. Gamma rays
    d. Microwaves

50. A block of 100kg of ice is melted into water. How much heat is needed to do this? Assume that the specific latent heat of fusion of ice is 340 kJ kg⁻¹.
    a. 294 J
    b. 34 000 J
    c. 294 000 J
    d. 34 000 000 J

51. Would you expect the amount of heat needed to change this mass of water from the previous question into water vapour to be more or less than the amount of heat you have calculated above?
    a. More, because the distance between gas particles are greater than the distance between liquid particles
    b. More, because gas particles are larger than liquid particles
    c. Less, because heat had already been supplied from melting the ice
    d. Less, because the surrounding air is hotter now

52. Explain why we feel cooler after a shower.
    a. Our minds are more refreshed, so it is a psychological consequence
    b. Our bodies have less germs, so our skin is more exposed to the air
    c. The water molecules take energy from our skin to evaporate
    d. We absorb cool energy from the surroundings

53. When our skin is rubbed with an alcohol swab, the area feels cool. When our skin is rubbed with a swab soaked in water, we feel nothing out of the ordinary. Why?
    a. Alcohol has a chemical that reacts with our skin to make us feel cold
    b. Alcohol is more volatile
    c. Water has no chemical reaction with our skin
    d. Water is absorbed by our skin whereas alcohol is not

54. Ice skaters sharpen the blades of their skates frequently. Why?
    a. To increase the pressure they exert on the ice so the melting point will increase
    b. To decrease the pressure they exert on the ice so the melting point will increase
    c. To increase the pressure they exert on the ice so the melting point will decrease
    d. To decrease the pressure they exert on the ice so the melting point will decrease

55. Carpeted floors feel warmer than non-carpeted floors. Why?
    a. They are made of material with high heat capacity
    b. They are made of poor convectors of heat
    c. They are made of poor conductors of heat
    d. They are made of poor radiators of heat

8 Waves, Sound [__ / 30]

1. Pick the false statement. All electromagnetic waves..
   a. Can travel through a vacuum
   b. Are not made of particles
   c. Travel slower than sound
   d. Travel at the same speed

2. Which statement best describes a sound wave?
   a. It is transverse
   b. It travels slower than light
   c. The direction of its particles is parallel to the direction of propagation of the wave
   d. It does not require a medium to travel

3. Which is correct?

	Highest frequency		Lowest frequency
a.	Gamma rays	Yellow light	X-rays
b.	Violet light	Blue light	Red light
c.	Microwaves	UV rays	X-rays
d.	Radio waves	UV light	Infra red

4. Which is correct?

	Longest wavelength		Shortest wavelength
a.	Gamma rays	Yellow light	X-rays
b.	Violet light	Blue light	Red light
c.	Microwaves	UV rays	X-rays
d.	Radio waves	UV light	Infra red

5. Which is incorrect?
   a. Computers emit gamma rays
   b. X-rays are used to treat cancer
   c. The sun emits infra red rays
   d. Mobile phones emit microwaves

6. Which of the following waves can be longitudinal?

    I   slinky
    II   sound
    III   ocean

    a. I only
    b. II only
    c. I and II only
    d. I, II and III

7. Which of the statements below is true about a transverse wave and a longitudinal wave traveling in the same direction?
    a. The amplitude of the transverse wave is always larger
    b. The frequency of the transverse wave is always higher
    c. The directions of their motions are parallel
    d. The directions of their motions are perpendicular

8. Which property can differentiate the wave used to kill cancer cells and the wave from a siren?
    a. Colour
    b. Direction of motion
    c. Direction of propagation of particles
    d. Amplitude

9. A and B are two points on a slinky. When a wave passes through the slinky, there is a 2s gap between the first and second vibration at point A and a 9s gap between the first vibration at point A and the first vibration at point B. The wavelength of this wave is 3m. What is the velocity of this wave?
    a. 1.5 m/s
    b. 6 m/s
    c. 18 m/s
    d. 27 m/s

10. In the situation above, what is the distance between A and B?
    a.   0.33 m
    b.   2 m
    c.   3 m
    d.   4.5 m

11. A cork is floating in the sea. How does it move?

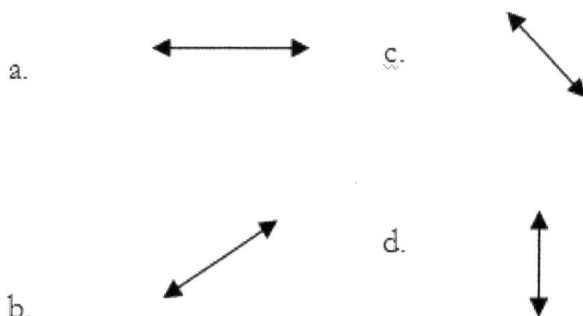

a. $\longleftrightarrow$

c. $\searrow$

b. $\nearrow$

d. $\updownarrow$

12. Which statement is true about a radio wave and a gamma wave?
    a.   In a vacuum, a radio wave travels faster than a gamma wave
    b.   Radio waves have shorter wavelengths than gamma waves
    c.   Gamma waves have a lower frequency than radio waves
    d.   A radio wave is transverse and a gamma wave is not longitudinal

13. Which graph can be used to find the amplitude of a microwave?
    a.   Displacement-distance graph
    b.   Distance-time graph
    c.   Velocity-time graph
    d.   Velocity-distance graph

14. Which property of a gamma wave can be seen from its displacement-time graph?
    a. Velocity
    b. Frequency
    c. Period
    d. Wavelength

15. What is a wavefront?
    a. An imaginary line connecting the crests of a wave
    b. An imaginary line connecting the crests and troughs of a wave
    c. The particle at the beginning of a wave
    d. The particle at the end of a wave

16. What is the speed of this water wave, given that it takes 2.4 seconds for it to move from one arrowhead to the other?

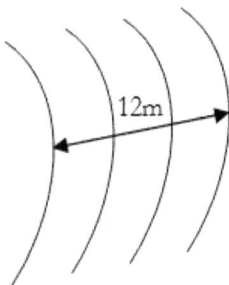

12m

    a. 2.4 * 12
    b. 0.8 * 0.4
    c. 1/0.8 * 0.4
    d. 0.8 * (1/12)

17. The wave below is moving towards the left. In which directions are the particles moving?

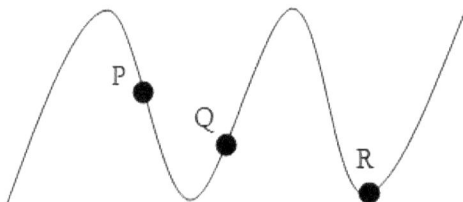

	P	Q	R
a.	Left	Left	Left
b.	Down	Up	At rest
c.	Right	Right	Right
d.	Up	Down	At rest

18. As a water wave moves from the deep ocean to the shallower shore, what happens?
    a. Velocity decreases
    b. Frequency decreases
    c. Wavelength increases
    d. The direction of the wave bends

19. A detector on a boat uses sound waves of 330 m/s to detect fish. A man sends out a wave and receives the signal 2 seconds later. How far away is the fish?
    a. 165 m
    b. 330 m
    c. 660 m
    d. 1320 m

20. The same man in the previous question sends a wave with the same detector to locate his friend 2km away. How long does it take for his friend to receive his signal?
    a. 2 s
    b. 3.1 s
    c. 6.1 s
    d. 12.2 s

21. Why are humans not able to hear dog whistles?
    a. The amplitude of the sound waves emitted is too high
    b. The speed of the sound waves emitted is too high
    c. The wavelength of the sound waves emitted is too high
    d. The frequency of the sound waves emitted is too high

22. A man and a dog stand between 2 walls. They are facing each other. The dog barks. The man hears the bark, the first echo and the second echo 1 second, 4 seconds and 8 seconds after the bark respectively.

    Where are the possible positions of the man and the dog?

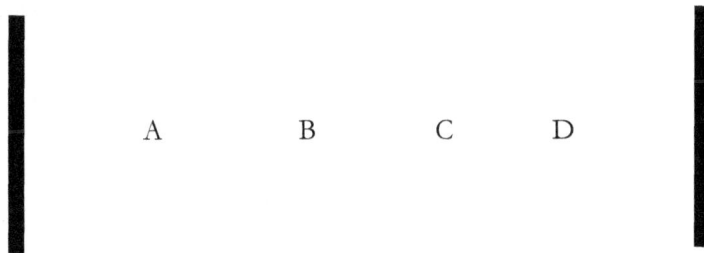

    A   B   C   D

	Man	Dog
a.	Position A	Position D
b.	Position D	Position A
c.	Position D	Position B
d.	Position C	Position B

23. Following from the previous question, when will the dog hear the first echo?
    a. After 4 seconds
    b. After 5 seconds
    c. After 10 seconds
    d. After 13 seconds

24. Following from the previous question, if the man screams, when will the dog hear the first echo of the scream?
    a. After 1 second
    b. After 3 seconds
    c. After 4 seconds
    d. After 5 seconds

25. When will the dog hear the second echo of the scream?
    a. After 6 second
    b. After 8 seconds
    c. After 9 seconds
    d. After 13 seconds

26. A man stands between 2 walls. He lets out a short scream. He hears an echo after 2 seconds, and then a second echo after 5 seconds. How many seconds after his scream does he hear the 7th echo?
    a. 9
    b. 35
    c. 17
    d. 49

27. In a sound wave, the distance between a region of compression and its successive region of rarefaction is…
    a. ½ λ
    b. λ
    c. 1.5 λ
    d. 2 λ

28. Using the information below,

Displacement / m

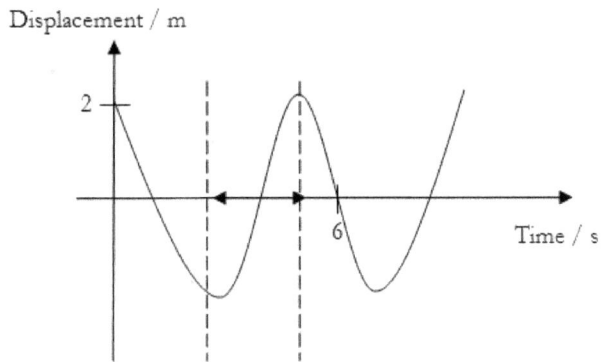

Displacement / m

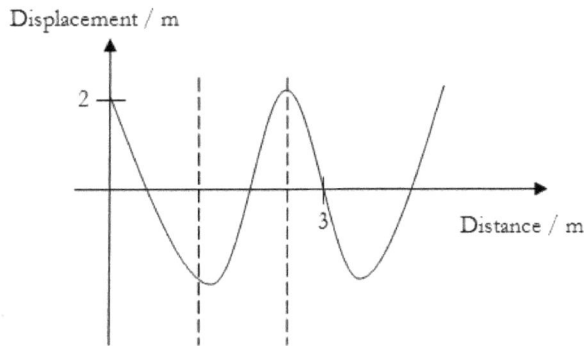

What does the arrow represent?
   a. Period
   b. Wavelength
   c. Half the period
   d. Half the wavelength

29. What is the frequency of the wave?
   a. 1/3 Hz
   b. 1/2 Hz
   c. 1/4 Hz
   d. 1/6 Hz

30. If the wavelength doubles and the frequency remains constant, what is the velocity of the wave?
    a. 0.5 m/s
    b. 1 m/s
    c. 2 m/s
    d. 3 m/s

9 Lenses, Reflection, Refraction [__ / 30]

1. A converging lens has a focal length of 30 m. When an object is placed 60 m away from it, the image observed is
   a. Real, upright, diminished
   b. Real, inverted, magnified
   c. Real, inverted, same size
   d. Virtual, upright, same size

2. A beam of light is shone from air into substance q, then into substance x. Find the refractive index of substance q and substance x.

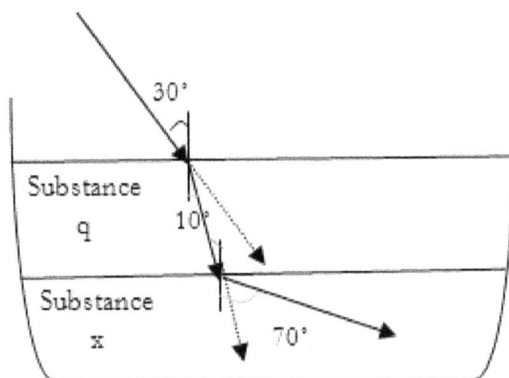

	n of substance q	n of substance x
a.	0.35	0.18
b.	0.35	5.41
c.	2.88	0.18
d.	2.88	5.41

3. A convex lens projects a sharp image on a screen. The screen is now shifted back and the image becomes blurred. What can be done to get a sharp image again?
   a. Shift the lens towards the screen
   b. Shift the object towards the lens
   c. Shift the object away from the lens
   d. Shift the lens away from the screen

4. A converging lens has a focal length F. To use this lens to focus sunlight to set a leaf on fire, what is the best distance between the lens and the leaf?

     a.   0.5 F

     b.   F

     c.   1.5 F

     d.   2 F

5. A woman of height 1.5m wants to see her entire image in a standing mirror. What is the shortest length of mirror that will enable her to achieve this?

     a.   1.00m

     b.   1.25m

     c.   1.50m

     d.   3.0m

6. Light travels at a speed of 1.65×10^8 ms^{-1} in substance x. Given that the speed of light in a vacuum is 3.0×10^8 ms^{-1}, find the refractive index of substance x.

     a.   0.55

     b.   1.1

     c.   1.82

     d.   3 64

7. A beam of light is shone into a glass block. Given that the refractive index of glass is 1.5, find angle x.

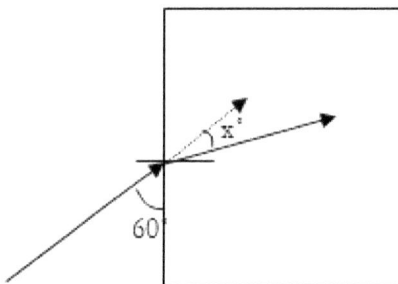

     a.   14.6

     b.   24.7

     c.   25.4

     d.   35.3

8. Given that the refractive index of water is 1.33, find the speed of light in water.
   a. $1.33 / 3.0 * 10^8$
   b. $1.33 * 3.0 / 10^8$
   c. $1.33 / 3.0 / 10^8$
   d. $1.33 * 3.0 * 10^8$

9. Joan and Joanna are standing in front of a plane mirror with Joanna standing 30cm behind Joan and 50cm from the mirror. How far away is Joanna's image from Joan?
   a. 20cm
   b. 50cm
   c. 70cm
   d. 100cm

10. The observed image of an object is slightly smaller than the actual object when the object is placed 11 m away from a converging lens. The image appears to be larger when the object is shifted such that it is now 9 m away from the lens. What is the focal length of the lens?
    a. 5 m
    b. 10 m
    c. 15 m
    d. 20 m

11. A light beam travels from substance X to air. What is the refractive index of substance X?

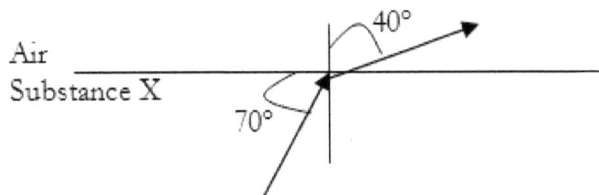

   a. $\sin 70° / \sin 40°$
   b. $\sin 30° / \sin 40°$
   c. $\sin 40° / \sin 30°$
   d. $\sin 70° / \sin 20°$

12. Total internal reflection will occur when

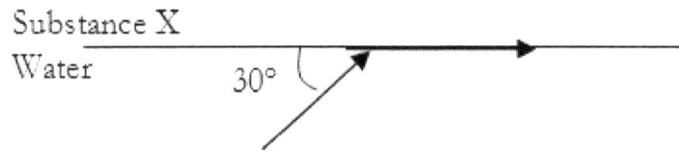

Substance X
_____
Water   30°

a. The angle of incidence exceeds 30°
b. The angle of incidence is smaller than 30°
c. The angle of incidence exceeds 60°
d. The angle of incidence is smaller than 60°

13. Which is not a possible characteristic of an image formed through the lens of a photocopier?
a. Virtual
b. Magnified
c. Diminished
d. Inverted

14. 3 rays of light travel from substance Y to substance X. The following diagrams show what happened in an earlier experiment.

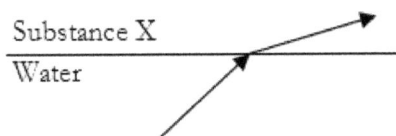

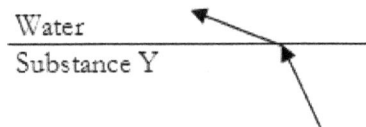

Substance X
Water

Water
Substance Y

What will happen to the 3 light rays shown below as they move from substance Y to substance X?

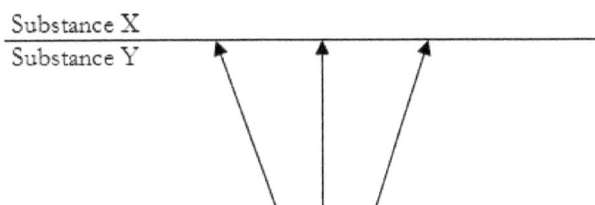

Substance X
Substance Y

	Left arrow	Middle arrow	Right arrow
a.	Bends right	Bends left	Does not bend
b.	Bends left	Bends right	Does not bend
c.	Bends right	Does not bend	Bends left
d.	Bends left	Does not bend	Bends right

15. In the experiment above, when is total internal reflection not likely to occur?
   a. When light passes from substance Y to water
   b. When light passes from water to substance X
   c. When light passes from substance Y to substance X
   d. When light passes from substance X to substance Y

16. In the experiment above, when is total internal reflection most likely to occur?
    a. When light passes from substance Y to water
    b. When light passes from water to substance X
    c. When light passes from substance Y to substance X
    d. When light passes from substance X to substance Y

17. Where will the image be seen?

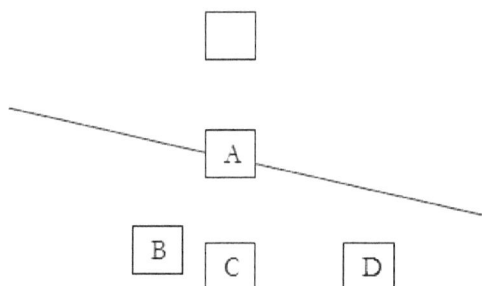

    a. B
    b. C
    c. D
    d. A

18. A ray of light passes from glass to plastic. It does not bend. Why?
    a. Glass and plastic have the same refractive index
    b. Glass and plastic have the same density
    c. The angle of incidence is $0°$
    d. The angle of incidence is $90°$

19. A converging lens is used to form an image exactly the same size of the object. If the image is 5cm away from the lens, what is the distance between the object and the image?
    a. 5 cm
    b. 10 cm
    c. 15 cm
    d. 20 cm

20. Following on from the previous question, the object is now moved 3 cm towards the lens. What happens to the image?
    a. It becomes smaller
    b. It becomes larger
    c. It moves away from the lens but the size remains the same
    d. It also moves towards the lens but the size remains the same

21. A girl peeps through a hole at the 30cm mark of a metre ruler into a 40cm long mirror. Which portion of the ruler is she able to see in the image?

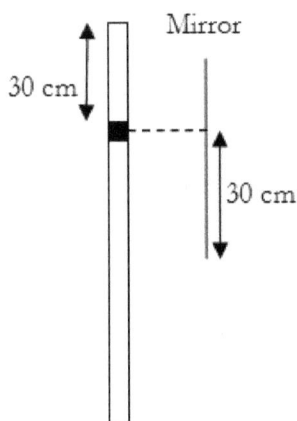

    a. From the 10cm mark to the 60cm mark
    b. From the 10cm mark to the 90cm mark
    c. From the 20cm mark to the 60cm mark
    d. From the 20cm mark to the 90cm mark

22. Which is a possible characteristic of an image formed through the lens of a converging lens with a focal length of 6cm, when the object is 13cm away from the lens?
    a. Inverted
    b. Magnified
    c. Virtual
    d. Same size

23. An object is 3cm tall. Through a magnifying glass, it appears to be 9cm tall. What is the distance between the image and the magnifying glass if the distance between the object and the lens is 2cm?

     a. 0.67cm
     b. 4.5cm
     c. 6cm
     d. 8cm

24. Which property of optical fibres enables them to be used for their purpose?

     a. They are light
     b. They are made of material of high refractive index
     c. They are transparent
     d. heir surfaces are painted with a coat of mirror

25. A man throws a spear to kill a fish, but he misses. Why is it so?

     a. The spear refracts when it passes through the water
     b. The fish appears closer to the man than it actually is
     c. The fish appears further away from the man than it actually is
     d. Light refracts when it passes from the man's eye to the fish

26. Can student A see student B in the mirror, and vice versa?

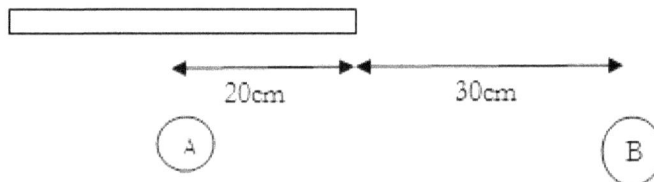

     a. A and B can see each other
     b. A can see B, B cannot see A
     c. B can see A, A cannot see B
     d. A and B cannot see each other

27. In the situation above, how must student B move such that he will be visible to student A?
    a. 5cm to the left
    b. 10cm to the left
    c. 15 cm to the left
    d. 20cm to the left

28. In the same situation as above, if student B were to move such that he is now standing directly behind student A and student A is facing the mirror, what will happen? Assume they are the same height.
    a. A and B can see each other
    b. A can see B, B cannot see A
    c. B can see A, A cannot see B
    d. A and B cannot see each other

29. Which statement is true
    a. Light must always refract when it passes from one medium to another
    b. Light will never refract when it passes through a curved surface
    c. The ratio of the speed of light in a vacuum to the speed of light in a medium represents the medium's refractive index
    d. The refractive index can always be found using the formula $n = \sin i / \sin r$

30. An image on a screen is not clear. What could be the reason?
    a. The light rays are not converging at the screen
    b. The image formed is virtual
    c. The light rays have bounced off the screen
    d. Half the lens is obstructed

10 Current Electricity, D. C. Circuits [__ / 40]

1. If wire X has twice the resistance of wire Y and has a radius that is one third of wire Y's radius, what is the ratio of the resistivity of wire X and wire Y?
    a. 1 : 3
    b. 2: 3
    c. 1: 9
    d. 2: 9

2. Which of the following is most correct about the resistance in ammeters and voltmeters?

	Ammeter	Voltmeter
a.	High	Low
b.	High	High
c.	Low	High
d.	Low	Low

3. A battery delivers 10 000 J of energy to a 20W rice cooker. How long will the cooker run before the battery dries up?
    a. 500 minutes
    b. 200 000 minutes
    c. 500 seconds
    d. 200 000 seconds

4. Bulbs A and B are connected in parallel. Bulb A is in series with a thermistor and bulb B is in series with a light dependant resistor. What happens if the temperature suddenly increases and the lights go off?

	Bulb A	Bulb B
a.	Brighter	Brighter
b.	Brighter	Dimmer
c.	Dimmer	Brighter
d.	Dimmer	Dimmer

5. What is a rheostat used for?
    a. To break the circuit when the current gets too high
    b. To break the circuit when the voltage gets too high
    c. To adjust the resistance of a circuit
    d. To adjust the resistivity of the wires in a circuit

6. A parallel circuit has 10 branches with a resistor in each branch. A new branch with a 2Ω resistor is added. What happens to the voltage of the entire circuit?
    a. Increases by 2V
    b. Decreases by 2V
    c. Does not change
    d. Impossible to tell

7. A single bulb in a series circuit with a resistance of 3Ω has a rating of 6V. What is the charge passing through it in 1 second?
    a. 2C
    b. 20C
    c. 18C
    d. 180C

8. Which circuit has the lowest resistance? Assume all resistors are identical.

a.

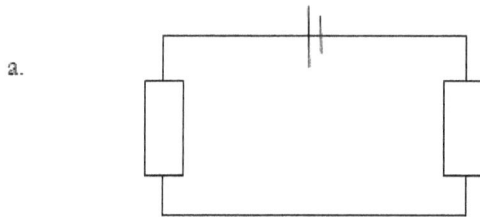

b.

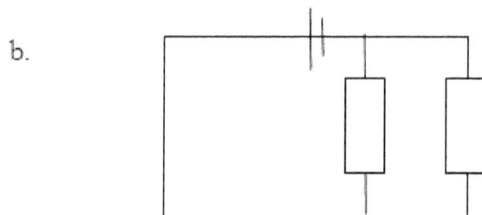

c.

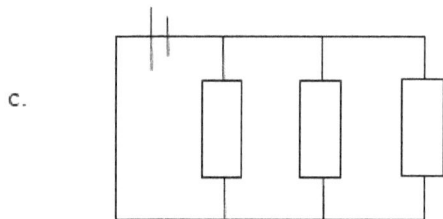

d.

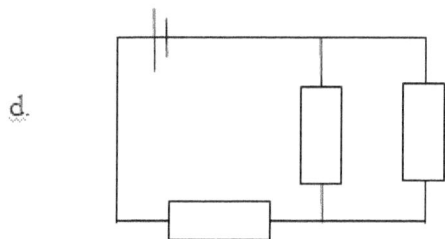

9. Which of the following is correct about the connection of Ammeters and Voltmeters?

	Ammeter	Voltmeter
a.	Series	Series
b.	Parallel	Parallel
c.	Parallel	Series
d.	Series	Parallel

10. What happens to the readings in V, A1 and A2 when the surrounding temperature increases?

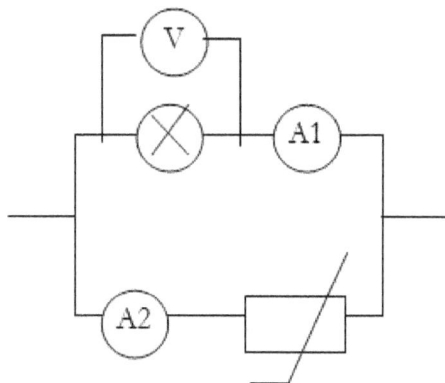

	V	A1	A2
a.	Decreases	Increases	Increases
b.	Decreases	Decreases	Increases
c.	Increases	Increases	Decreases
d.	Increases	Decreases	Decreases

11. Substance X has a resistivity of 1.23. It is used to make a wire that is 30cm long with a diameter of 3mm. What is the resistance of the wire?

    a. $1.23 * 30 / (\pi * 0.003^2)$
    b. $1.23 * 0.3 / (\pi * 3^2)$
    c. $1.23 / 30 / (\pi * 3^2)$
    d. $1.23 * 0.3 / (\pi * 0.003^2)$

12. 2 bulbs with negligible internal resistance are connected in parallel with a dry cell that has an e.m.f. of 12V. What is the current passing through each bulb if the effective resistance of the circuit due to the wires is R?

    a. $12/R$
    b. $6 * R$
    c. $6/R$
    d. $24R$

13. What is the power rating of each bulb in the circuit described above?

    a. $36/R$
    b. $2R$
    c. $72/R$
    d. $6R$

14. If the efficiency of a bulb rated 240V, 75W is 75%, what is the work done by it in converting electrical energy to heat and light energy when it is used for 10 minutes?

    a. $240 * 0.75 * 10$
    b. $75 * 0.75 / (10 * 60)$
    c. $240 * 0.75 * 10 * 60$
    d. $75 * 0.75 * 10 * 60$

15. The backlight of an iphone automatically gets brighter when it is under sunlight. How?

    a.   There is a thermistor that decreases its resistance when there is light
    b.   There is a light dependent resistor that decreases its resistance when there is light
    c.   There is a thermistor that increases its resistance when there is light
    d.   There is a light dependent resistor that increases its resistance when there is light

16. An air-conditioner is automatically switched off when the air reaches a certain temperature. It is then switched on again when the room temperature increases. How?
    a. There is a thermistor that decreases its resistance when there is light
    b. There is a light dependent resistor that decreases its resistance when there is light
    c. There is a thermistor that increases its resistance when there is light
    d. There is a light dependent resistor that increases its resistance when there is light

17. Explain how a variable resistor is used to control the brightness of stage lights.
    a. The resistance is lowered to increase the brightness of the stage lights and vice versa
    b. The resistance is lowered to decrease the brightness of the stage lights and vice versa
    c. The resistance is increased to increase the brightness of the stage lights and vice versa
    d. The resistance is increased to decrease the brightness of the stage lights and vice versa

18. A bulb has a rating of 6V. What does this mean?
    a. It provides 6J of energy per second
    b. It provides 6J of energy for every charge that passes through it
    c. It allows a current of 6A per unit of resistance
    d. It can overcome 6Ω of resistance with every unit of current

19. Which device allows us to manually control the brightness of a light bulb?
    a. Thermistor
    b. Light dependent resistor
    c. Rheostat
    d. Fuse

20. Which graph(s) correctly depicts Ohm's Law?

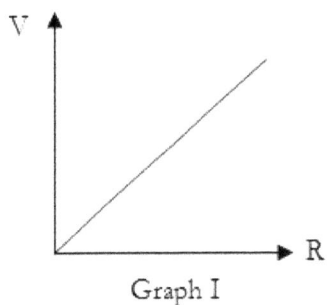

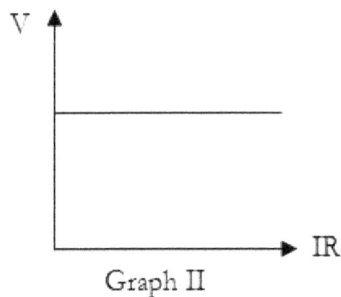

Graph I

Graph II

  a.   Graph I only
  b.   Graph II only
  c.   Graph I and Graph II
  d.   Neither Graph I nor Graph II

21. A single bulb in a series circuit with a resistance of 3Ω has a rating of 6V. What is the charge passing through it in 30 seconds?
  a.   60C
  b.   540C
  c.   600C
  d.   1800C

22. Which is the correct definition of power?
  a. $P = E\,t$
  b. $P = I\,R$
  c. $P = Q\,V$
  d. $P = Q\,V\,/\,t$

23. The gradient of the graph represents...

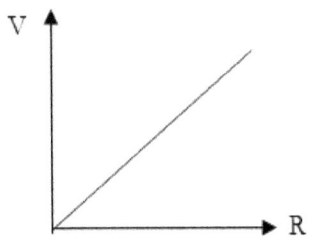

    a.   Charge
    b.   Current
    c.   Resistivity
    d.   Power

24. A1 registers a current of 2.5 A.

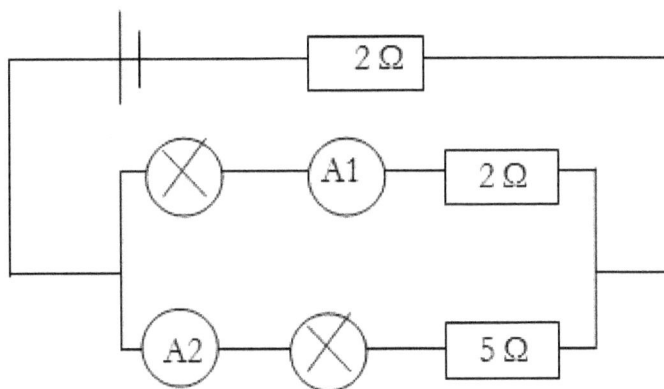

Find the reading in A2.

    a.   1A
    b.   2.5 A
    c.   5 A
    d.   5.2 A

25. What is the e.m.f. of the battery of the circuit in the previous question?

      a.   2 V
      b.   5 V
      c.   7 V
      d.   13 V

26. According to the circuit drawn below,

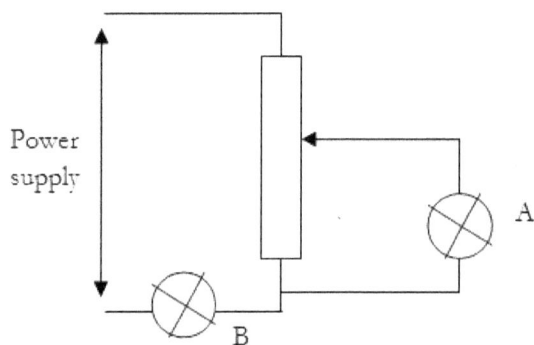

What changes can be observed in light bulb A as the slider is gradually moved upwards?

      a.   It gets brighter
      b.   It gets dimmer
      c.   There is no change in the brightness
      d.   It flicks on and off periodically

27. Referring to the same diagram in the previous question, what happens to light bulb B?

      a.   It gets brighter
      b.   It gets dimmer
      c.   There is no change in the brightness
      d.   It flicks on and off periodically

28. The area under the graph represents..

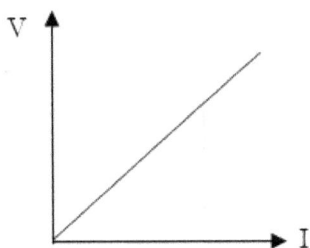

a. Power
b. Energy
c. Resistance
d. Charge

29. The slider is moved to the right. What happens to the bulbs?

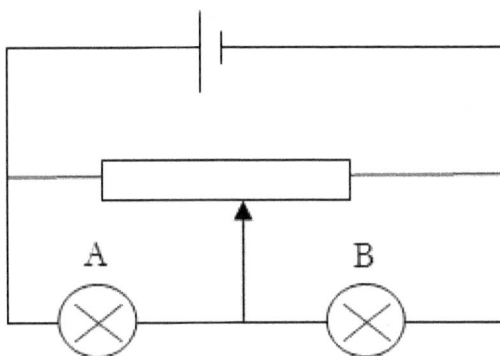

	A	B
a.	Brighter	Brighter
b.	Brighter	Dimmer
c.	Dimmer	Brighter
d.	Dimmer	Dimmer

30. The slider is moved to the right. What happens to the bulb and the ammeter? The bulb does not have negligible resistance.

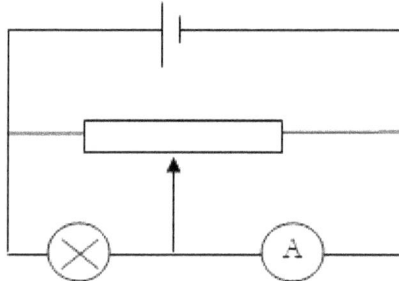

	A	B
a.	Brighter	Lower reading
b.	Brighter	No change
c.	Dimmer	Higher reading
d.	Dimmer	No change

31. Which change to a circuit could cause a bulb in it (connected in series) to glow more brightly?
    a. Add a resistor
    b. Use a longer wire
    c. Add a fuse
    d. Use a thicker wire

32. The graph of current against voltage of a bulb is found to be as shown below. Why does the bulb not obey Ohm's law that resistance and current should have a linear relationship?

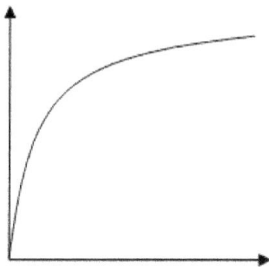

    a.   When current decreases, the increased temperature causes resistance to increase

    b.   When current decreases, the increased temperature causes resistance to decrease

    c.   When current increases, the increased temperature causes resistance to decrease

    d.   When current increases, the increased temperature causes resistance to increase

33. There is a circuit as shown below.

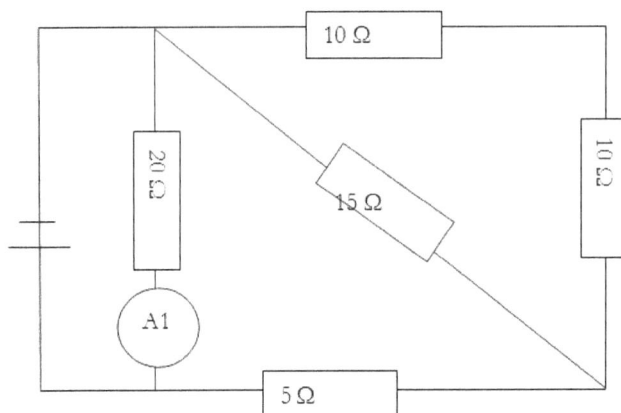

10 Ω

20 Ω

15 Ω

10 Ω

A1

5 Ω

Find the effective resistance of this circuit.

    a.   6.4 Ω
    b.   8.1 Ω
    c.   12.7 Ω
    d.   60 Ω

34. The current in A1 reads 5A. What is the e.m.f. of the battery?
    a.   4 V
    b.   50 V
    c.   80 V
    d.   100 V

35. What is the potential difference across the 5 Ω resistor?
    a.   5 V
    b.   28 V
    c.   37 V
    d.   100 V

36. Which graph shows the correct relationship?
    Y-axis: Resistance; X-axis: Cross-sectional area

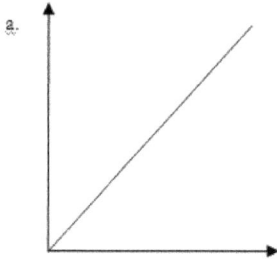

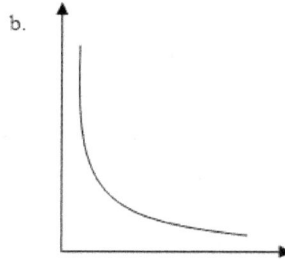

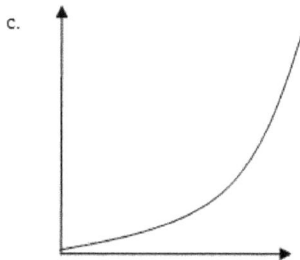

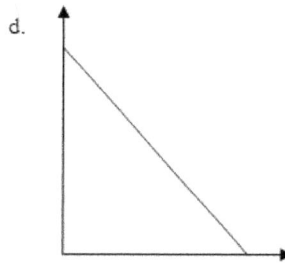

37. A wire is carrying a current of 200A and the resistance in it is 10Ω. What is the cost of the power loss if each unit of electricity costs $0.12?
    a. $0.24 / second
    b. $24 / second
    c. $0.48 / hour
    d. $48 / hour

38. A parallel circuit has 10 branches with a resistor in each branch. A new branch with a 2Ω resistor is added. What happens to the resistance of the entire circuit?
    a. Increases by 2Ω
    b. Decreases by 2Ω
    c. Increases by less than 2Ω
    d. Decreases by less than 2Ω

39. Which graph shows the correct relationship?
    Y-axis: Resistance; X-axis: Length

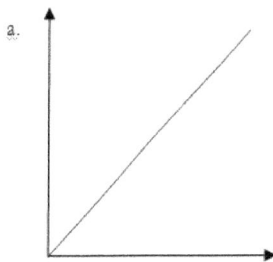

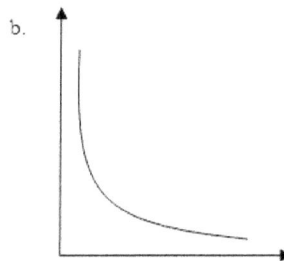

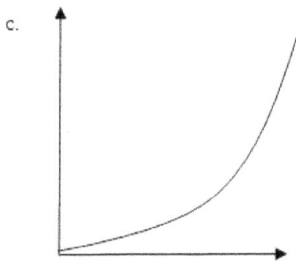

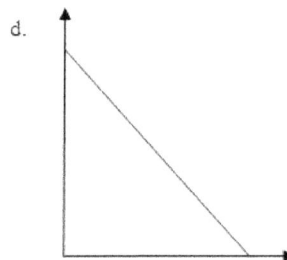

a.

b.

c.

d.

40. Which graph shows the correct relationship?
    Y-axis: Resistance; X-axis: Cross-sectional radius

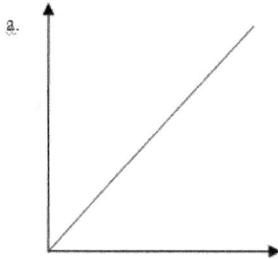

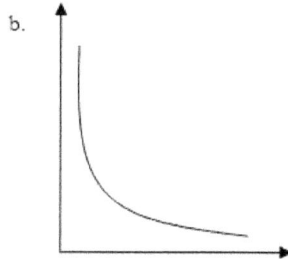

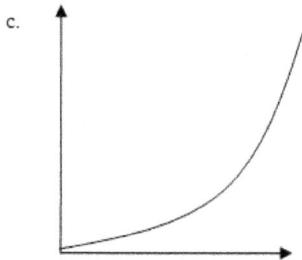

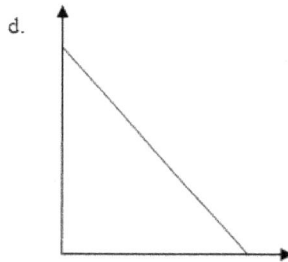

a.

b.

c.

d.

11 Static Electricity [__ / 30]

1. What happens when we touch a positively charged metal ball?
    a. Electrons flow from the ball to us
    b. Electrons flow from us to the ball
    c. Nothing happens
    d. Electrons flow both ways

2. A charged pith ball attracts another pith ball. Which of the following must be true?
    a. The second pith ball must carry an opposite charge
    b. The second pith ball does not necessarily have to be charged
    c. The second pith ball has fewer charges than the first pith ball
    d. The second pith ball is smaller than the first pith ball

3. What happens when a negative charge is placed in an electric field?
    a. It becomes neutralized
    b. It becomes more strongly charged
    c. A force acts on it in the direction of the field
    d. A force acts on it in the opposite direction of the field

4. A charged polythene ball is discharged by
    a. Earthing it
    b. Bringing an oppositely charged ball near it
    c. Heating it over a flame
    d. Bringing a magnet near i
        t

5. A polythene rod is rubbed with a cloth. The rod becomes negatively charged. How does this happen?
    a. Electrons move from the cloth to the rod
    b. Electrons move from the rod to the cloth
    c. Protons move from the cloth to the rod
    d. Protons move from the rod to the cloth

6. Which of the following figures is most likely to be correct?

a.

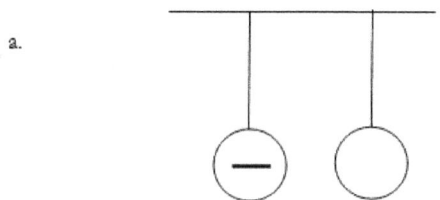

b.

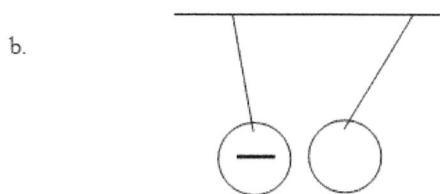

c.

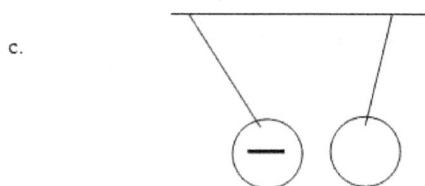

d.

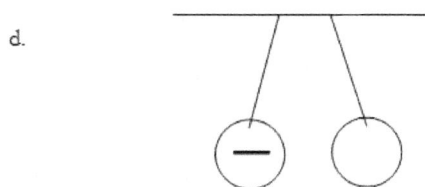

7. A small conducting ball hangs on a nylon thread between 2 oppositely charged metal plates. What happens to the ball when it is given a slight negative charge?

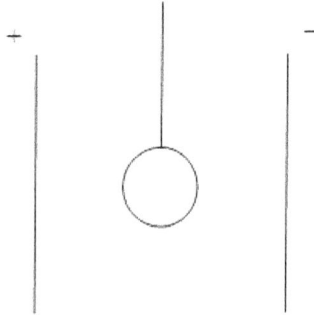

    a. It moves to the left, touches the plate and sticks there
    b. It moves to the right, touches the plate and sticks there
    c. It moves to the left and then back and forth continuously, touching the plates
    d. It moves to the right and then back and forth continuously, touching the plates

8. A copper rod is rubbed similarly with a cloth. What happens and why?
    a. The rod becomes negatively charged because it gains electrons from the cloth
    b. The rod becomes positively charged because it loses electrons from the cloth
    c. The rod is not charged as it gains both protons and electrons from the cloth
    d. The rod is not charged as it is a conductor and any charge will be conducted away

9. A conducting sphere is charged through induction. Why does it have to be placed on an insulating stand?
    a. Because it's standard procedure
    b. To prevent any excess positive charges from flowing to the surroundings
    c. To prevent any excess negative charges from flowing to the surroundings
    d. It has to be raised in order to be earthed

10. The metal spheres are on insulating stands. They are separated while the rod is still in place. Then rod is then removed. What are the final charges carried by metal spheres X, Y and Z?

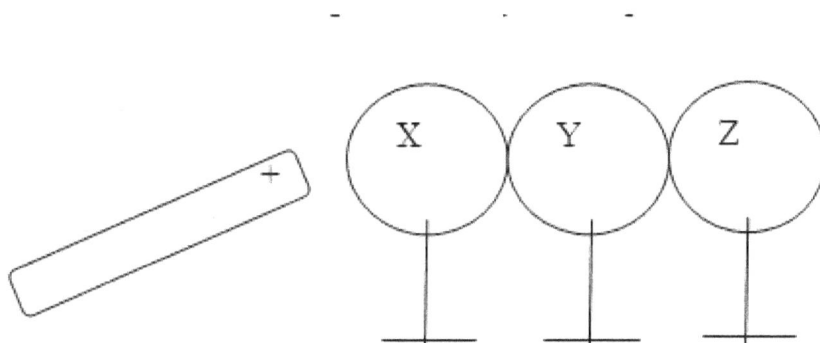

	X	Y	Z
a.	negative	neutral	positive
b.	positive	neutral	negative
c.	negative	slightly positive	positive
d.	positive	slightly negative	negative

11. The current in a circuit is measured to be 0.48A. Given than the charge of an electron is 1.6×10^{-19} C, how many electrons are flowing through any fixed point in the circuit at a point in time?
    a. 3×10^{18} electrons
    b. 5×10^{18} electrons
    c. 7×10^{18} electrons
    d. 9×10^{18} electrons

12. In which direction does negatively charged particle X move?

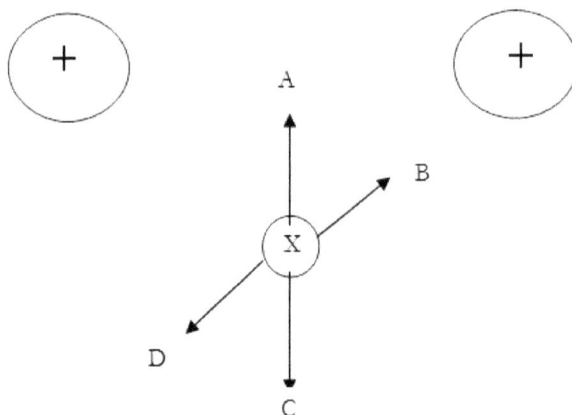

  a. C
  b. D
  c. B
  d. A

13. A positively charged metal ball suspended freely from an insulating thread is brought near to an uncharged metal sphere on an insulating stand. They do not touch each other. Explain what happens.

  a. Protons in the sphere move towards the side of the sphere facing the charged ball

  b. Protons in the sphere move away from the side of the sphere facing the charged ball

  c. Electrons in the sphere move towards the side of the sphere facing the charged ball

  d. Electrons in the sphere move away from the side of the sphere facing the charged ball

14. What are the final charges carried by the metal ball and the metal sphere in the previous question after they are brought together such that they are in contact?

	Ball	Sphere
a.	Negative	Neutral
b.	Positive	Neutral
c.	Positive	Positive
d.	Neutral	Negative

15. A positively charged metal rod is brought close to a metal sphere on an insulating stand. They do not touch. Which diagram accurately shows the final charge distribution?

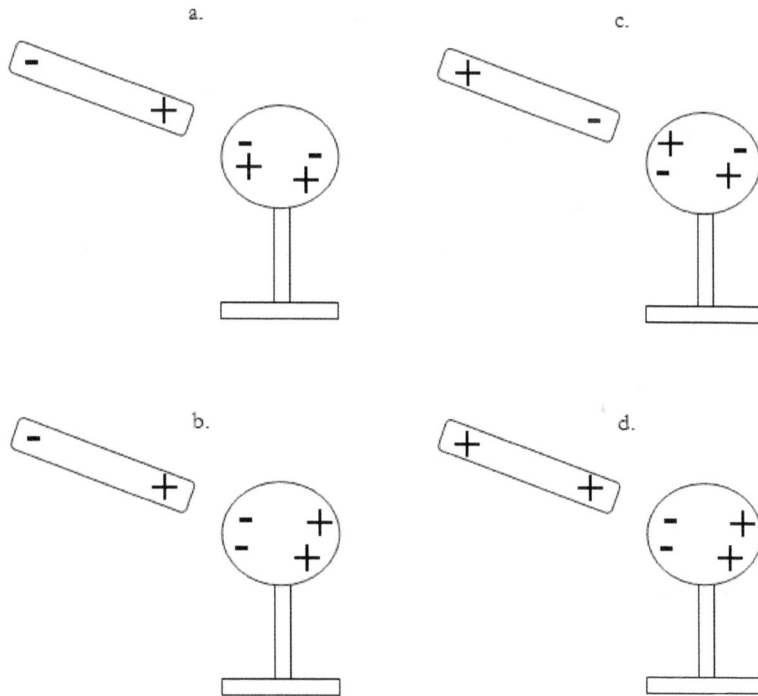

16. The metal sphere in the previous question is earthed. What is the new charge distribution after the earthing wire is removed?

	Rod	Sphere
a.	Negative	Neutral
b.	Positive	Neutral
c.	Positive	Negative
d.	Neutral	Negative

17. The metal sphere in the previous question is brought close to a neutral metal sphere such that they touch. The neutral metal sphere is found to have gained a negative charge. Explain what happened.
    a. Electrons move from the first sphere to the second sphere
    b. Protons move from the second sphere to the first sphere
    c. Neutrons move from the first sphere to the second sphere
    d. Nucleons move from the second sphere to the first sphere

18. A positively charged metal sphere is connected to a neutral metal sphere of half the size. What happens?
    a. There is a negative charge induced in the smaller sphere
    b. The smaller sphere becomes positively charged, but less than the larger sphere
    c. Both the spheres are now equally charged
    d. The positive charge in the larger sphere is neutralized and both spheres are now neutral

19. When there are excess positive charges in the clouds, lightning is formed. How does lightning work?
    a. There is an electric current flowing from the sky towards the ground
    b. There is an electric current flowing from the ground towards the sky
    c. Excess positive charges flow to the ground
    d. Excess positive charges flow from the ground

20. What does the electric field of a charged hollow sphere look like?

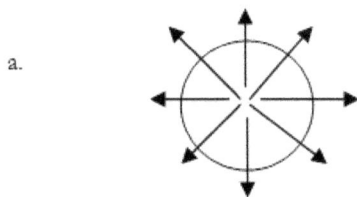

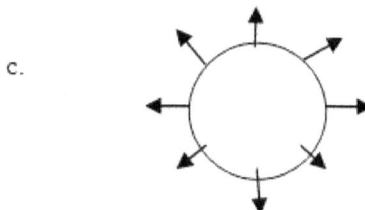

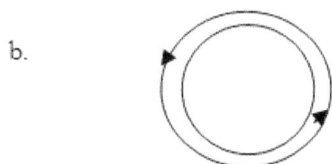

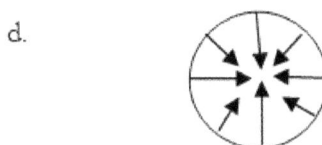

a.

c.

b.

d.

21. Which statement is false
    a. Electrostatics can be dangerous as well as useful
    b. Conductors cannot be charged by rubbing
    c. Insulators cannot be charged
    d. Touching a charged object with bare hands will cause a small electric shock

22. How does the use of electrostatics help in the application of spray paints?
    a. It is cheap
    b. It is safe
    c. It makes the paint spread out evenly
    d. It makes the paint colour stay longer before fading

23. What happens when a charged object is earthed?
    a. Electrons flow from the earth to the object
    b. Electrons flow from the object to the earth
    c. Electrons flow either from the object to the earth or the other way
    d. Electrons and protons flow either from the object to the earth or the other way

24. Balls A and B are charged insulators suspended freely by nylon threads. Which of the following statements must be true?

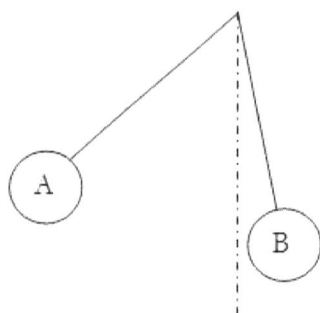

    a.   Ball A is lighter than ball B
    b.   Ball A carries a smaller charge than ball B
    c.   Ball A carries a larger charge than ball B
    d.   The two balls are oppositely charged

25. Name a useful application and a hazard of electrostatics.

	Application	Hazard
a.	Photocopier	Suffocation
b.	Lightning	Pollution
c.	Spray paint	Photocopier
d.	Flue-ash removal	Lightning

26. When electrons flow from one object to another..
    a.   A current is generated that flows in the same direction as the electrons
    b.   A current is generated that flows in the opposite direction from the electrons
    c.   The charges neutralize each other such that both objects become uncharged
    d.   A current is generated that flows in the same direction as the electrons

27. Electric field lines
    a. Point towards objects that have negative charges
    b. Must be curved
    c. Are stronger if they are thicker
    d. Are made of electrons

28. Electroscopes are used for
    a. Detecting positive charges only
    b. Detecting negative charges only
    c. Detecting either positive or negative charges
    d. Detecting heart beats

29. What happens when the two objects touch?

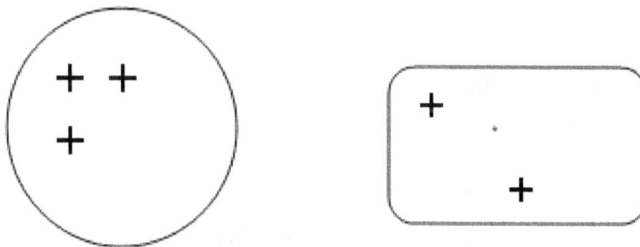

    a. They will never touch as they repel each other
    b. Both will end up electrically neutral
    c. Both will remained positively charged
    d. The circle will have a positive charge, the rectangle will have a negative charge

30. Which is not a consequence of electrostatics
    a. Explosions
    b. Lightning
    c. Radiation
    d. Fertilizer sprays

12 Practical Electricity [__ / 15]

1. The switch must always be connected to the
   a. Live wire, so that the appliance will not be live when switched off
   b. Earth wire, because it will direct all the current to the earth
   c. Neutral wire, so that people will not get electrocuted
   d. Live wire, if not the switch will not work

2. An electric plug
   a. Must have 3 pins
   b. Must have 2 pins
   c. Only has 1 pin
   d. Can have either 2 or 3 pins

3. Fuses
   a. Must be connected to the neutral wire
   b. Must be connected to the earth wire
   c. Must be connected to the live wire
   d. Can be connected to any wire

4. The plug to a heater has a 20A fuse. When the heater works normally, it draws a current of 18A. a dog has chewed the wire such that the live wire now makes contact with the earthed metal casing. What happens?
   a. The heater explodes when switched on
   b. Anybody who touches the metal casing will get electrocuted
   c. When the switch is turned on, the fuse blows and breaks the circuit
   d. The heater cannot be turned on anymore

5. A cooker of power rating 3000W is used for 5 hours. If the total cost of powering the cooker came up to $0.30, what is the cost of electricity?
   a. 10 cents per kWh
   b. 15 cents per kWh
   c. 25 cents per kWh
   d. 50 cents per kWh

6. A kettle draws a current of 10A under normal conditions. It is connected to a fuse of rating 12A. As the kettle gets old, it becomes faulty. It starts to draw a current of 15A when switched on. What happens when a 15A current is drawn?
    a. The fuse blows and the current is cut off
    b. People get electrocuted when they touch the kettle
    c. The kettle explodes
    d. The fuse melts and reduces the current back to 10A

7. To rectify the problem described in the previous question, the fuse is replaced with another one with a 17A rating. What happens when the kettle is switched on now?
    a. It draws a current of 17A
    b. It still draws a current of 15A
    c. People get electrocuted but the fuse remains intact
    d. The fuse blows and there is no risk of electrocution

8. Was the solution above appropriate in fixing the situation?
    a. Yes, because the kettle is now safe to use
    b. No, because the kettle is still drawing a dangerous current
    c. No, because the current drawn increased instead of decreasing
    d. Yes, because it saves money from not having to replace the fuse

9. Which is correct?

	Earth wire	Live wire	Neutral wire
a.	Green & yellow	Blue	Brown
b.	Brown	Green & yellow	Blue
c.	Blue	Brown	Green & yellow
d.	Green & yellow	Brown	Blue

10. Both circuit breakers and fuses can be used to protect appliances. When is it more favourable to use a circuit breaker?
    a. When the current is high
    b. When the current is low
    c. When the current fluctuates
    d. When the budget is low

11. Both circuit breakers and fuses can be used to protect appliances. When is it more favourable to use a fuse?
    a. When the current is high
    b. When the current is low
    c. When the current fluctuates
    d. When the budget is low

12. How many 240V, 20W bulbs can be connected in parallel across a 6A fuse?
    a. 40
    b. 72
    c. 800
    d. Infinite

13. How many 240V, 20W bulbs can be connected in series with a 6A fuse?
    a. 40
    b. 72
    c. 800
    d. Infinite

14. Which statement is true?
    a. Electrical appliances require an earth wire, a live wire and a neutral wire to work
    b. A fuse that has melted cannot be reused
    c. Double insulation is necessary for all appliances
    d. Circuit breakers are used in place of fuses in order to save money

15. When birds stand on wires with high voltages, they don't get electrocuted. However, if a human were to accidentally touch the same wire, he will surely die. Why?
    a. Birds have a special coating on their feet
    b. Humans are better conductors of electricity because we have a higher water content
    c. Humans are earthed while birds are not
    d. Birds have high resistance because of their feathers

13 Magnetism & Electromagnetism [__ / 25]

1. A beam of electrons is shot between the opposite poles of magnets. What happens?
    a. The beam deflects towards the north pole
    b. The beam deflects towards the south pole
    c. The beam deflects into the plane
    d. The beam deflects out of the plane

2. Two wires are placed side by side. Currents are run through the wires in opposite directions. What is observed?
    a. The wires are attracted to each other
    b. The wires repel each other
    c. The wires do not move
    d. There is not enough information given to determine what happens to the wires

3. A magnet is pushed halfway into one side of the coil and then pulled out. What is observed?

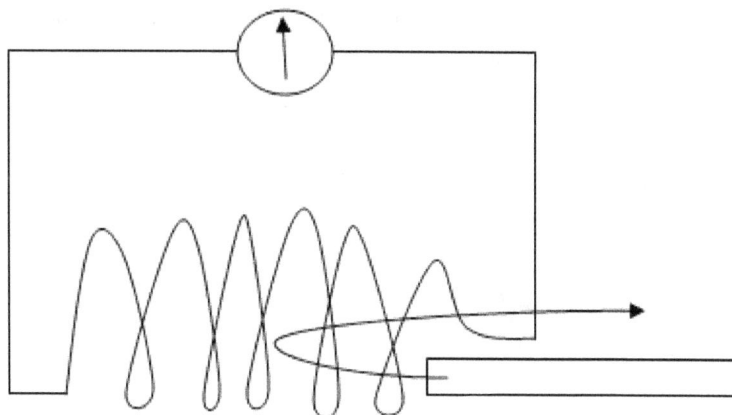

    a. The needle of the galvanometer deflects in one direction and stays there
    b. The coil is repelled
    c. The needle of the galvanometer deflects in one direction and then in the other direction
    d. A current is induced in the circuit

4. A galvanometer's needle points
    a. In the direction of conventional current flow
    b. In the direction of electron flow
    c. Towards the north pole of a bar magnet
    d. Towards the south pole of a bar magnet

5. A straight wire is moved vertically downwards to cut the magnetic field lines between oppositely charged magnetic poles. What happens?
    a. A force is induced
    b. A current is induced
    c. A magnetic field is formed
    d. Heat energy is induced

6. In an a.c. generator, what happens when the strength of the magnetic field increases?
    a. The motor spins faster
    b. The coil slows down
    c. The current induced increases
    d. The current changes direction

7. A closed circuit consists of a coil, a galvanometer and no battery. The north pole of a bar magnet is pushed into the coil. What will be observed as the bar magnet is being pushed in?

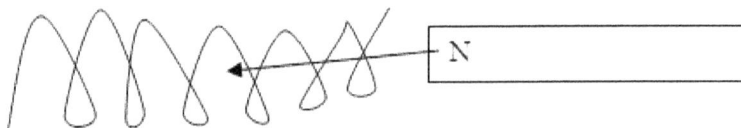

    a. The needle of the galvanometer deflects and stays there
    b. The needle of the galvanometer deflects and then returns to its original position
    c. The needle of the galvanometer deflects and starts to oscillate
    d. The needle of the galvanometer does not move

8. What happens in a d.c. motor when the thickness of the wire is increased?
   a. The coil rotates faster
   b. The coil rotates slower
   c. The strength of the magnetic field increases
   d. The strength of the magnetic field switches direction

9. Which statement is true?
   a. A transformer must have more turns in the primary coil than in the secondary coil
   b. A transformer must be supplied with a dc current
   c. A transformer's core must be made of a magnetic material
   d. A transformer's core must be made of an electrical conductor

10. What happens in an a.c. generator when the coil rotates at a higher speed?
   a. The strength of the magnetic field increases
   b. The strength of the magnetic field switches direction
   c. The current induced increases
   d. The current changes direction

11. What is the function of a split ring commutator?
   a. To convert a D.C. into an A.C.
   b. To maintain constant electrical contact
   c. To ensure a continuous rotating motion
   d. To induce magnetism

12. Which is a magnetic material?
   a. Copper
   b. Brass
   c. Zinc
   d. Cobalt

13. A bar magnet drops vertically through a coil attached to a galvanometer. What happens to the needle of the galvanometer?

    a. Deflects, goes back to its original position, then deflects in the opposite direction
    b. Deflects, goes back to its original position, then deflects in the original direction
    c. It oscillates periodically until the entire magnet is out of the coil
    d. It does not move

14. The graph below shows how the voltage of the output of an a.c. generator varies with time

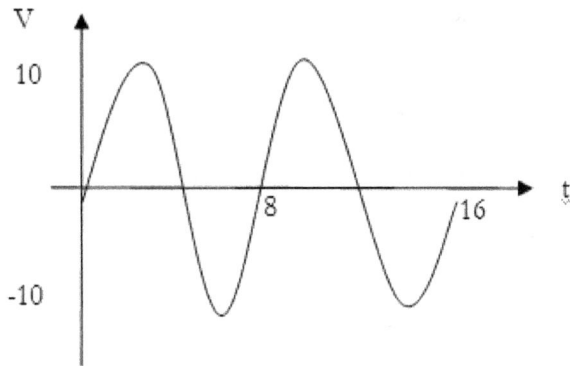

Which dotted line shows what will happen if the generator is made to rotate in the opposite direction at half the original speed?

a.
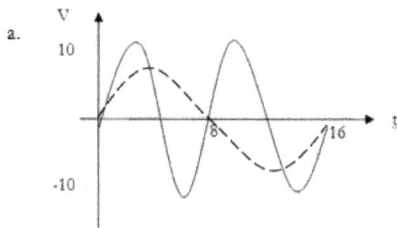

c.
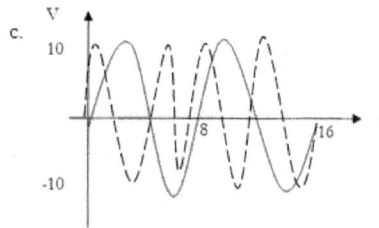

b.
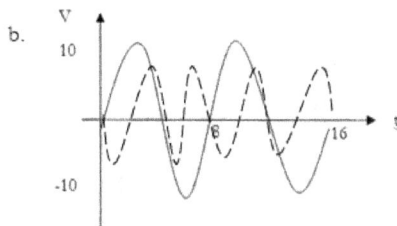

d.
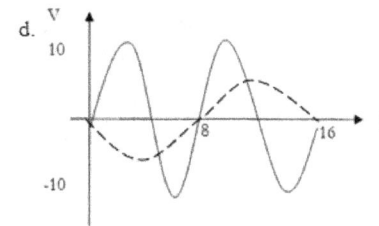

15. From the previous question, which dotted line shows what will happen if the coil is made to rotate at twice the speed and the magnetic field strength halves?

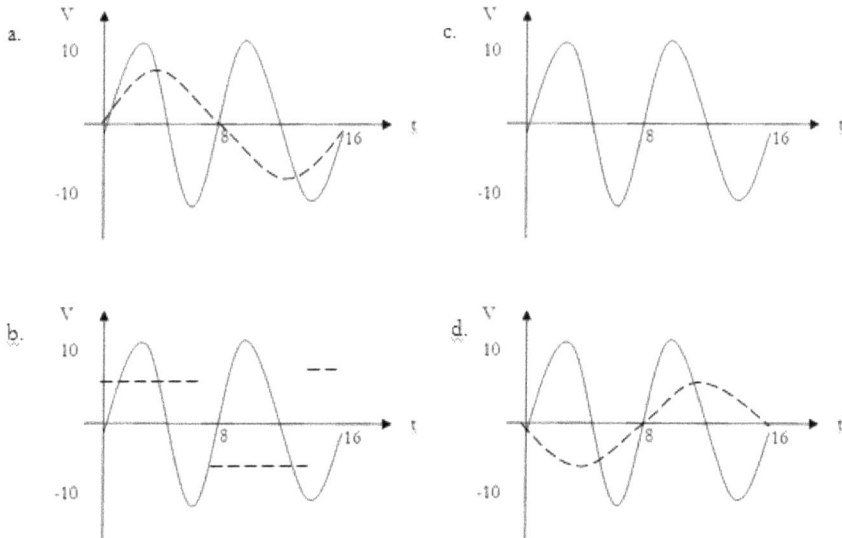

16. What is a diode used for?
    a. To increase the resistance when the temperature drops
    b. To increase the resistance when the light goes off
    c. To force the current in a particular direction
    d. To control the voltage of a circuit

17. Which statement is false?
    a. The current supplied to a transformer must be alternating
    b. Transformers can be step-up or step-down
    c. Transformers can be used to change voltage and current
    d. Eddy currents increase the efficiency of transformers

18. The magnetic field lines are out of the plane of the paper. Which diagram shows the correct path of a proton (solid line) and an electron (dotted line) being shot towards the right?

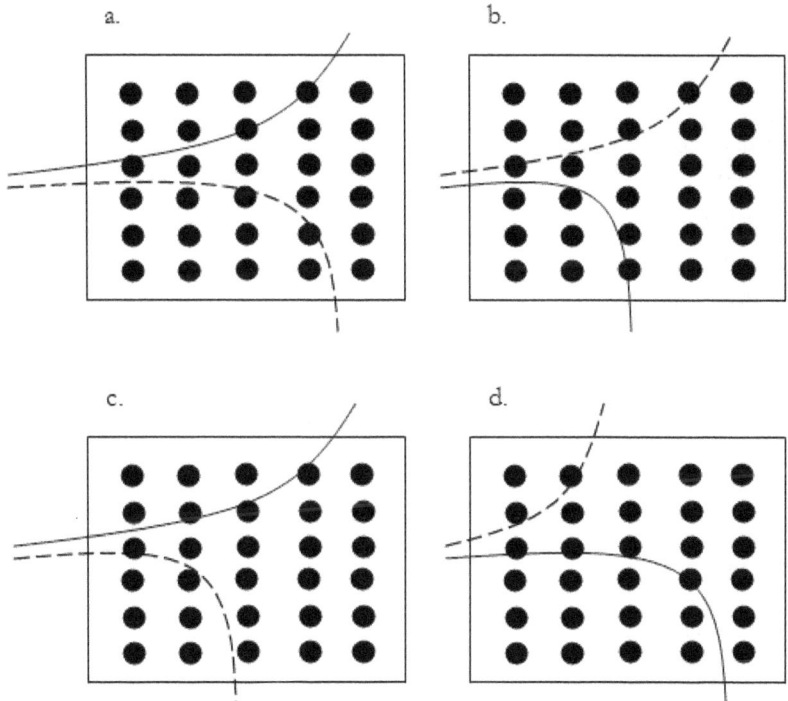

19. A transformer has 10 turns in its primary coil. It is supplied with a 20V d.c. and has 500 turns in its secondary coil. What is the voltage across its secondary coil?
    a. 0 V
    b. 25 V
    c. 1000 V
    d. 20 000 V

20. A transformer has 10 turns in its primary coil. It is supplied with a 20A a.c. and has 500 turns in its secondary coil. What is the current in its secondary coil, assuming 80% efficiency?
   a.   0.32 A
   b.   0.40 A
   c.   800 A
   d.   1000 A

21. Why are high voltages used to transmit electrical power?
   a.   Reduce power loss
   b.   It is cheaper
   c.   It is faster
   d.   It is safer

22. What are the directions of the needles in compasses X, Y and Z?

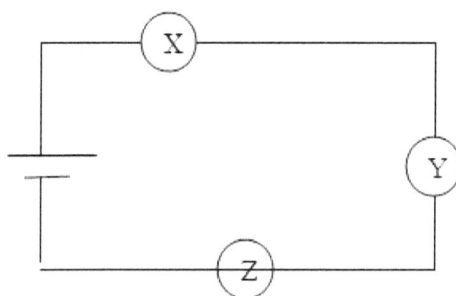

	X	Y	Z
a.	Up	Right	Down
b.	Down	Left	Up
c.	Down	Left	Down
d.	Right	Up	Left

23. What will happen when a split ring commutator is removed from a d.c. motor?
    a.   The coil will stop moving
    b.   The coil will change rotating direction every 360°
    c.   The coil will change rotating direction every 180°
    d.   The coil will change rotating direction every 90°

24. What will happen when the carbon brushes are removed from an a.c. generator?
    a.   The current produced will be d.c. instead of a.c.
    b.   There will be no current produced
    c.   The wires will get entangled
    d.   The coil will not move in a single direction but start to oscillate periodically

25. If an object is a permanent magnet, then it must be
    a.   Attracted to the end of a compass needle
    b.   Attracted to the tip of a compass needle
    c.   Able to attract another permanent magnet
    d.   Repelled by one end of a compass needle

www.ingramcontent.com/pod-product-compliance
Lightning Source LLC
Chambersburg PA
CBHW050354100426
42739CB00015BB/3390